SURVIVAL AND SUCCESS

THE TRUE STORY OF A LUFTWAFFENHELFER

A MEMOIR
Part 1: The European years
(1932–1949)

*To my dear friend Wei-Kao Lu
with best compliments.*

10/1/2024

NICHOLAS STANDISH

ABOUT THE AUTHOR

Nicholas Standish, of Russian descent, was born in Yugoslavia. In 1944, at the age of twelve, he was drafted into the German air force as a Luftwaffenhelfer starting in Eger, Sudetenland (now Cheb, the Czech Republic). After many harrowing near death incidents, including being shot for sabotage, WW2 ended for him in Salzburg, Austria. There he was moved many times from one DP (Displaced Persons) camp to another, starting in Saalfelden and ending in Asten near Linz. From there he migrated to Australia in 1949 as an assisted migrant. After working the compulsory two years for the Australian government in the NSW Railways and then the Electricity Commission, he entered academia. He became a Professor of the University of Wollongong. Later he became a Resident Professor in Cilegon, Indonesia. He finished his 25 years of Indonesian time in January 2017.

Published in Australia by Sid Harta Publishers Pty Ltd,
ABN: 46 119 415 842
23 Stirling Crescent, Glen Waverley, Victoria 3150 Australia
Telephone: +61 3 9560 9920, Facsimile: +61 3 9545 1742
E-mail: author@sidharta.com.au

First published in Australia 2017
This edition published 2017
Copyright © Nicholas Standish 2017
Cover design, typesetting: WorkingType (www.workingtype.com.au)

Standish, Nicholas
Survival and Success: The true story of a Luftwaffenhelfer. A Memoir
Part 1 : The European years (1932–1949)
ISBN: 978-1-921030-83-3
pp142

ACKNOWLEDGEMENTS

First, I wish to thank my wife and children for encouraging me — and then putting up with my writing memoirs.

Second, all my experience of writing has been the writing of academic scientific reports and research papers. Naturally my memoirs read just like a scientific report. This was pointed out to me by my son Peter and my son-in-law the Reverend Father Charles Balnaves.

Third, I wish to thank Veronica Epstein, the Line Editor for Sid Harta Publishers, for her skill and dedication in making my scientific-report-reading-memoir, read like normal memoirs!

Fourth, thanks are also due to Luke Harris of Working Type Studio for alerting me to a few typos and errors of fact.

Luftwaffenhelfer: an explanation

At the end of 1942 in Germany, 16 years old school boys were drafted as Luftwaffenhelfers to operate anti-aircraft guns. Later (1944/5) these German 'child soldiers' were sent to the German frontline fighting units and their places filled with boys as young as 10, from other countries, such as Latvia, Estonia, Lithuania, Poland, Yugoslavia, etc. It may be of interest to remark that one German boy who started as a Luftwaffenhelfer and then later sent to the frontline was Joseph Ratzinger. He later became Pope Benedict XVI. My own example is Dr-Ing Karl Heinz Peters, Director Thyssen Stahl. I met him and became his friend in 1978. His experience paralleled that of Joseph Ratzinger.

PROLOGUE

'Sabotage!! Sabotage!! You will be shot,' yelled the duty guard officer while at the same time contorting his face, making him look like a monster I had seen in a horror movie, and also rapidly moving the stiffened palm of his hand across his throat in a cutting action that gave a meaning of certainty to his words. The guards and the uniformed office staff present nodded their heads indicating their full agreement with the officer's decision.

The date was 23 December 1944 and the place was the German Luftwaffe complex, a military airfield and barracks in Eger, Sudetenland, Germany (now Cheb, Czech Republic).

I was a twelve and half year old 'Luftwaffenhelfer', or 'German Airforce Helper', stationed in the complex and wearing a Luftwaffe uniform that was at least three sizes too big.

I had just been brought to the guardhouse to join my two fourteen year old friends who were actually caught running away from the military aircraft from which we were unscrewing some instrument panel lamps, while I escaped back to the barracks.

I will never forget that frosty, starry December night. First, running away at what must have been superman speed from the German military aircraft guards who were yelling 'Halt, Halt, wir shiessen!' ('Stop, Stop, or we shoot!'). A few hours later I was marched away from my barracks, the snow squeaking under our boots as we walked, and was finally shoved into an unbearably hot, cigarette smoke filled guardhouse, with its red potbelly stove in the middle radiating heat in all directions. This mean-looking duty officer and his guards were standing there—all clearly ready to explode at us and shoot us then and there, if for no other reason than as a lesson to the few thousands boy soldiers of many

1

nationalities and of different ages in the complex at that time. Any activity that has not been approved beforehand is not to be even contemplated, and definitely not attempted!

What happened at the end of the day—or rather, night—is to be found later on in the memoirs, as I believe that to fully appreciate and understand these unbelievable things —and more importantly, accept their credibility that they actually happened—we must know three things:

Firstly, why was I, a Yugoslavian-born boy of twelve and half years, there in the German airforce uniform, in the first place?

Secondly, how did I get there, so many countries away from where I was born and where I spent my early years of a happy childhood?

And finally, how is it that some 60 years later I am alive to tell this story when at the time there was no doubt that we were to be shot?

What follows is my life story that provides the answers to these questions, plus many other near-misses of being killed or blown up in ships, trains, on roads or in buildings.

CHAPTER I

My Story Begins

I was born in Novi Sad, Yugoslavia in the province of Bachka—the former Hungarian part of the Austro-Hungarian Empire, on 12 April 1932 and named Nikolai Stanishewski, the latter being the family name.

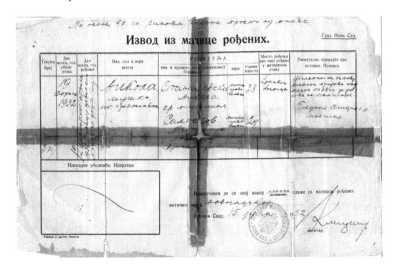

My birth certificate

The family consisted of my father, also Nikolai, my mother Natalia and my brother, Sergei, seventeen months my senior.

Both my parents were born in Russia. They were what was known as the 'White Russians', that is, émigrés of the Russian Revolution of 1917 when the communists, also known as 'Red Russians' or 'Bolsheviks', took over and disposed of the Tsar Nikolai II and his family.

The terms 'White Russian' and 'Red Russian', as well as their military equivalents of 'White Army' and 'Red Army', derive from the colours of their flags: red used by the communist 'Bolsheviks' and the traditional white colour of the tsars for the monarchist 'White Russians'.

My father's birth certificate

My father was born in Kursk in 1892, or more precisely *near* Kursk in a town called Schigri and therefore shares the same birthplace, if not the actual year, with Nikita Khruschev, the first ruler of Russia after Stalin. Khruschev was faintly inclined towards democracy and famous for taking his shoe off and banging it on the table in the United Nation Assembly to show how strongly he disagreed with President John Kennedy's ideas.

My father was one of six children of a businessman with interests in the herring trade. Since salted herrings have always been—and still are—an integral part of traditional Russian cuisine, my father belonged to a relatively well-to-do family. Hence, he was able to enrol in the Law Faculty in St Petersburg University and pay all his fees and lodgings and, presumably, also afford the many extra-curricular activities known to have been a mandatory part of the students' life at that time.

Father's record book as a student in the Law Faculty of the Imperial University in St Petersburg, starting 21 August 1914.

The start of World War I and the subsequent Revolution cut

short his studies in St Petersburg. Like the then many patriotic students loyal to the monarchy, he joined the White Army in the cavalry regiment and fought in many places, including the infamous Lemnos in Greece where he was wounded, requiring 11 months of recuperation.

When the fighting ended and the communist revolutionaries with their Red Army took over the country and the government, all those unmistakably loyal to the monarchy and, of course, all those who fought with the White Army, fled to many parts of the world to await what most of them believed would be a quick return to Russia before the year was over, or soon after. Therefore, many thought it unnecessary and a waste of time to start afresh or do anything at all while waiting.

However, my father thought that he should continue his law studies so that he would not be a semester or two behind when he returned to Russia, and have to re-start at the point where the war interrupted his studies. So he first became a border guard at Triglav, meaning 'three heads' (a mountain) to earn money to pay his university fees. When he saved enough money he enrolled in the University of Zagreb and supported himself during his studies by washing dishes in the nearby restaurant.

As is known from history, the communist regime in Russia, or rather the Union of Soviet Socialist Republics (USSR) as it became formally, became strongly entrenched for the next 70 years until it was substituted by a democracy in 1991. Those still alive could finally now return. Not many did.

However, it should be remarked that some émigrés had returned in the late 1940s in response to an amnesty by the USSR government, steered by their own strong patriotism. It is widely known that most who returned then regretted it later.

My father completed his Doctor of Laws degree and joined the Yugoslav Public Service. I should note here that the testamur of my father's degree shown here is not only written in Latin as traditionally were all law degrees originating from the Roman Law, but also, though it is fully printed lithographically in a printing press, is but an official copy.

The original, also of course, fully professionally printed in a lithographic printing press was a much bigger document; without exaggeration the testamur itself measuring 80 x 50 cm and after framing, no less than 100 x 70 cm. It was no ordinary picture frame either, but an intricately carved one, and that was not all! At the bottom there was a round, intricately carved wooden box, of about 10 cm diameter, hanging by a short, fancy rope from the frame.

At this point it's a fair question to ask how I know all these intricate details of that testamur when it was lost during our moving house in 1940 and I was only eight years old then. Well, the answer is simple enough and my brother remembers it well, too. My father's work involved moving house many times and everywhere we moved, this big testamur was hung up in a prominent place in the lounge room. We boys were always intrigued by it, and especially so when we could read the words 'NOS REKTOR' which made us even more intrigued because we thought it had something to do with a nose; the word NOS being exactly the Russian word for a nose. Of course, what it actually means in Latin is 'WE THE RECTOR'. So, although we were told by our father never to touch the frame, let alone open the box, the curiosity was too much for us and we had to see what was this nose inside the box. Well, one day when we were alone in the house, we assembled enough courage to open the box. What was inside was the university seal embossed in a red sealing wax, so we took a knife and scratched away at the wax to find 'the nose'. Before we could destroy the seal fully, my father came home and on seeing what we had done, punished us severely—so severely, in fact, that it was impossible for us to ever forget the incident and the details leading to it.

My father's LLD testamur compared with my own PhD testamur

For the sake of comparing the old ways with the new ways, I submit a scanned copy of the testamur of my own doctor's degree from Otago University, New Zealand, in 1965.

Really pathetic! A standard A4 size paper with my name typed on it with a typewriter. No finesse, no fancy font, no intricacies and no carved box containing the university seal. I don't know what my two sons thought of it.

To be fair though, the Otago University testamurs before 1965 were a bit better. They were bigger (40 x 25 cm) and a bit fancier. What happened in 1965 was the appointment of a new Vice-Chancellor, Dr Arthur Beacham, an economist from UK with a reputation for savage cost cutting. His first cost cutting activity in Otago was the testamurs. I wonder how much money was saved and whether it was worth alienating so many graduates who, as alumni, were many years later asked for donations to the university.

Now, back to my father who had graduated with Doctor of

Laws (LLD) and joined the public service. His first posting was as 'Srezki Podnachelnik', or 'Assistant Head' of the small District of Novi Bechej—the latter being a small town where there was a small group of Russian émigrés and the 'Devichii Institut' or a Boarding School for Russian Girls.

Because it will come up later again, to understand what a 'Srezki Nachelnik', or District Head was, I explain it here.

For administrative purposes Yugoslavia of those days was divided into 'Banovina', with a 'Ban' heading its government and responsible to the Minister for Internal Affairs in the Central Government in Belgrade. In turn, a Banovina was divided into number of 'Srez's, headed by a 'Srezki Nachelnik' responsible to the Ban.

The above can be likened to something like our Australian states, with the State Premier (Ban) and shires or municipalities with their Shire President or Mayor (Srezki Nachelnik). The difference is that our Mayors and Shire Presidents are elected persons, doing the job part time as they often have other full time jobs, but a Srezki Nachelnik is a full time job and the person is an employee of the Public Service Department; in other words, he is a public servant.

Another difference is that a Srezki Nachelnik was in charge of the police, courts, railways, roads, etc. in his Srez. In other words, he was a little god. In this respect a more appropriate equivalent to a Srezki Nachelnik would be a District Commissioner of old in areas such as Northern Territory, Papua New Guinea, and such like.

I don't know how soon after my father's appointment as a Srezki Podnachelnik in Novi Bechej he met my mother, who was one of the pupils in the girls' school, but I know they were married on 1 September 1929.

My parents' marriage certificate

Soon after the wedding, my father was promoted to a much larger District of Novi Sad, still as a 'Srezki Podnachelnik', or 'Assistant Head'. Both my brother and I were born in Novi Sad.

My grandparents: Nikolai and Olga Saltikov

My thoughts now turn to my mother who was born in Kharkov, now Ukraine, in 1906, the only child of Nikolai and Olga Saltikov.

My grandfather was at that time, according to the inscription of an Analytical Geometry book he had written, an 'Ordinary' Professor of Mathematics in the local university. An interesting term, 'Ordinary', which is actually given to the higher category of professorship which holds a chair position, being superior to an 'Extraordinary' professor.

As to my grandmother, as far as I know, she attended to what is now called 'home duties', though with servants, gardeners, nannies, and the like, it is uncertain what such a term may mean.

After the 1917 Revolution, the Saltikovs, that is, my grandfather, my grandmother and my mother, who was then an eleven year old girl, escaped to Yugoslavia and settled in Belgrade. I say escaped rather than migrated for good reasons. One time when my brother and I, both in our early years of primary school, were visiting our grandparents in Belgrade with my mother, my grandfather took me and my brother into his study, closed the door and told us, in very slow and measured words his secret. Whether he asked us to never divulge it to anyone else, or not, I cannot remember. However, he must have impressed the secret very strongly on both of us as my brother and I remember it very well to this day.

Grandfather addressing conference ca 1950

My grandfather, who to us always looked stern, even now as I look at the photo of him delivering the keynote speech at an international conference of mathematicians in about 1950, said: 'Koka and Serjozha (using our diminutive names) you are our only grandchildren. When you are grown up and we are dead and the situation in Russia returns to normal you should go to our house in Mironossivskaya Street number 42 in Kharkov. It is a two storey house. Enter the front door and there before you, you will see the stairs leading to the upstairs. Lift the floor boards under those stairs to your right and there you will find a wooden box containing gold objects and precious stones. It is heavy, so be careful.'

Clearly, if the Saltikovs were leaving in the normal way with plenty of time, they would surely have taken the precious items with them, to help with their life in the new land. But no, they did not do that; they left the heavy box behind, almost certainly for fear it would slow down their escape.

[Note: Some 30 years later in 1970, I was in Moscow as a guest of the USSR Academy of Sciences and had my mind made up to travel to Kharkov to see what I could find. Unfortunately, rules concerning what visitors can, or cannot do, were very strict in those days so I did not make it. However, one evening in the dining room of my hotel I was with a group of scientists and in conversation I mentioned that my grandparents came from Kharkov. One of the older scientists was also from Kharkov and he asked me where in Kharkov they lived. When I said, 'In Mironossivskaya Street,' he said, 'Oh yes, I knew it, but it does not exist any more. Kharkov was heavily bombed during the war and that area was pretty well destroyed, so after the war they built a memorial park there'.]

In Yugoslavia my grandfather quickly became Professor of Mathematics in the University of Belgrade and settled in a two storey house in Varshavska Street number 36 in an area of Belgrade known as 'Profesorska Kolonia', or 'Professors' Colony'. Soon after the war (WW II), my grandfather, a geometer with publications on the subject in many learned magazines and as far as I know, was also a full member of the French Academy of Sciences. He started the first computing laboratory in Belgrade which expanded to become a Key Centre for Computing in Yugoslavia. All of this I was told by his staff and colleagues when I visited there in 1970. He must have been a man of some prominence, as there is a street in Belgrade that has been named after him, namely 'Ulitsa Nikolaja Saltikova' or 'Street Nikolaja Saltikova'

As to my mother, in line with something that seems to have been customary in those days, she was sent to a 'Devichi Institut', which as noted earlier, was a Russian boarding school for girls in Novi Bechej, a town some 120 km from Belgrade. Her class photo shows the girls in the school uniform, the wearing of which was mandatory at all times. (My mother is the third girl from the right in the front row.)

Institute class photo

Mother ca 1937

For comparison, a later photo shows my mother in 1937, wearing the then modern dress and the compulsory hat. Interestingly, as is seen in the class photo, the girls did not wear hats in school.

CHAPTER II

The Kosovo/Macedonia Years (1936 – 1941)

The family was in Novi Sad until the autumn of 1936. I was too young to remember much of the life in Novi Sad, except for a few hair-rising episodes that are firmly entrenched in my memory.

I will never forget a visit to the beach on the Danube one day in summer. It was always a favourite treat to go there for a swim and to build a few sand castles, but this day there was an added feature. A 'giant' ship (it had not one, or two, but fully three smoke-billowing funnels!) steamed through, creating huge waves that lashed the shore and frightened me no end! It was the largest structure I had ever seen, and I was left completely awestruck.

I also recall an idea of my father's to give us children a thrilling ride in a small two seater biplane (one seat behind the other). The plane was owned by his crazy Russian friend, who had most of his bones broken as a result of many emergency crash-landings of his plane in rocky fields and cow paddocks. In those days aeroplanes were flimsy contraptions, at best, that the God fearing folk believed were the devil's doing, as 'the good Lord never meant humans to fly—if He did, He would have provided them with wings'. Consequently, we were terrified and crying so much that my father decided to skip the idea of flying us around that day— or, ever for that matter!

In October 1936 the family moved from Novi Sad to Kachanik, a town in Kosovo, the Province that became ill-fated in the 1990s for the fierce fighting between Serbs and ethnic Albanians. Kachanik is also about 80 km from Skoplje, on a river, or rather a rivulet, called Lepenitsa, a tributary of the river Vardar which flows through Skopje, the capital of Macedonia.

Above I have used both 'Skoplje' and 'Skopje'. No, it is not a mistake. Macedonians say Skopje, especially after President Tito's death, and the region became an independent state. Before that time, and particularly when the region was part of the Kingdom of Yugoslavia when we were there, the city was officially named Skoplje with an 'L'. Actually, in the Cyrillic script 'LJ' is one letter — the 'soft-sounding L', whereas 'L' as such on its own is a 'hard-sounding L' and the two are quite different.

I remember well arriving in Kachanik, because we got there by train in the night and I was woken up when we arrived. Minutes after we began walking towards our new home an electrical storm started and I got scared. As my father began to walk faster, my brother and I could not keep up with him, so he picked both of us up rather strongly and started to essentially canter. And just as well, because the moment we got to our new home the heavens opened in a torrential downpour and so we had narrowly escaped getting drenched to the core.

Our move to Kachanik had been the result of my father's appointment as the 'Srezki Nachelnik' of the 'Kachanichki Srez'. The district consisted of the township of Kachanik itself with some 4,000 inhabitants or so, and a number of villages scattered over the hilly terrain of the Srez—the total inhabitants amounting to maybe some 10,000 people. As noted earlier, to all these people, who were mostly simple people of predominantly Muslim faith, my father was god!

We lived in a two storey government house, the only two storey house there, with a big garden and an impressive stone and metal fence. Of course, there was a full time gardener as well as

a cook, house servants and a nanny for us children. At the back
of our house was the local police station with its jail that looked
like a row of stables with the inmates being able to look from their
cells directly to the outside world. I remember the inmates making wooden spoons and toys for us children and passing them to
us through the small windows in their doors.

(left) Father's letter of appointment to Kachanik
(right) Father in Kachanik uniform

For our family, Kachanik was nothing short of a paradise. Our
life there was essentially one long holiday. Our house was the
meeting place for the local officials, like the stationmaster, the
town engineer, the agronomist, the veterinarian, the police chief,
the postmaster, the schoolmaster and others who constituted the
'cream of the Kachanik society'.

For the adults each week there seemed to have been a party of one sort or other in the house. As was the expected social grace of that period, the people at these gatherings spoke French—and badly at that! It would have been better and certainly would have prevented many misunderstandings and bad feelings, if they spoke Russian or Serbo-Croatian, as relevant. As to us children, we spoke both languages; generally Russian at home, which was our mother language and the Serbo-Croatian outside of the home.

When we went for walks with our mother, alone or with an accompanying nanny, women would bow and men would raise their hats to us. As most inhabitants were Muslims, the men wore white caps and the women wore shawls.

The main mosque, with its tall minaret, was not too far from our house and the call to prayer, five times per day as required by the Al Qur'an—the first at around 4 o'clock in the morning, and the last around 7 o'clock in the evening, was not a problem if the duty imam had a strong voice and the wind was in our direction. If the imam had a weak voice, or the wind was in opposite direction, or both, then we could not hear anything.

This is, of course, different from today with all manner of electronic wizardly, CD players, PA systems and the like, all of which combine so that at a flick of a switch decibels can be doubled, trebled, quadrupled and so on. And here I speak from first-hand experience, as in Cilegon, Indonesia where I have been on and off in the period 1992 – 2010, I live opposite a mosque with only 20 meters between us.

Actually, my son Peter can testify to the effect of PA. When he came for two days to visit me he was startled from his sleep—even though he was in the back bedroom—at 3 am (the imam misread his watch!) and again at 4 am.

(Above) View in front of the house looking at the mosque
(Below) Looking at the house from the mosque.
Housegirl standing at the gate

In the 1930s, especially in what now would be called a developing country, many parts of Yugoslavia were bereft of such electronic gadgets. Anyway, even if they were available they would not have been able to be used in Kachanik, because during our time there, there was no electricity, no running water or sewerage, and the roads were not paved.

Actually, the paving of the roads, was not a high priority at that time as all of the transportation in Kachanik was by donkeys and horse drawn carriages. The motor vehicles that passed through on their way to Skopje were very few and far between indeed. In fact, our dog, Caesar, a pedigree Doberman trained by my father to be obedient and also do all sort of tricks, could not be restrained from attacking these putt-putting and backfiring machines chugging their way through Kachanik. Poor Caesar had his left leg broken twice as it was caught under the front wheel of a vehicle. For some reason, Caesar always attacked front on, unlike modern dogs which go after the back wheels, if and when they attack cars at all.

As to the parties in our house, they were mainly held on weekends in daylight. If ever they were held in the evenings there was no problem as the lounge rooms were equipped with candelabras of kerosene lamps of the pump-up type, so they looked like the real electric lamps—except very much more dangerous if they caught fire! By the same token, heating of the house in the winter was by wood fire, as was the kitchen stove, and the bath water in the bathroom on bath days. Unlike the modern time, with its extravagant bathing or showering every day, in those days the practice can be summarised as: 'above the belt, below the belt and the whole', meaning wash only the upper part of the body one week, the lower part only the next week and have a bath on the third week. In winter time these weekly activities were generally extended to a ten day or a two week periods.

Our life in Kachanik ended in August 1937 when my father was appointed as the 'Politichno-Upravni Sekretari' of the 'Vardarska Banovina', i.e. akin to the Secretary of CIA—a big promotion for him, but also one that carried some danger with it. The term 'Banovina', it would be recalled, was akin to our state and 'Vardarska' simply means 'of the river Vardar', and identifies the region precisely, namely, the region we now know as Macedonia and Kosovo. The 'Ban' himself and all of the administrative departments and offices were located in Skopje, the capital of the 'Vardaksa Banovina'. So, my father was responsible for a wide area of land and his work was essentially that of the boss of the secret police, focusing on political activities (not politics), and embraced all manner of subversive activities against the state.

У ИМЕ

ЊЕГОВОГ ВЕЛИЧАНСТВА

ПЕТРА II

по милости Божјој и вољи народној

КРАЉА ЈУГОСЛАВИЈЕ

КРАЉЕВСКИ НАМЕСНИЦИ

НА ПРЕДЛОГ МИНИСТРА УНУТРАЊИХ ПОСЛОВА

указом од 5 августа 1937 године

III број 29675 поставили су

на основу §§ 45 от.3,48,9, ст. 1 тач. 1,103 ст. 1,846

Закона о чиновницима у вези §§ 42 тач.7,93 тач. 1 и 96

Финансијског закона за 1937/38 годину за политичко-управ-

ног секретара шесте групе Краљевске банске управе Вардар-

ске бановине Др. СТАНИШЕВСКОГ А. НИКОЛУ,среског начелни-

ка исте групе среза качаничког,по потреби службе.

К. III бр. 27134
16 августа 19 37 год.
Београд.

По наредби
Министра унутрашњих послова,
В.Д. Начелник,
Саветник,

Father's letter of appointment to Skopje

Although when my father was the 'Srezki Nachelnik' in Kachanik he had a revolver and a short sabre with a fancy handle as part of his ceremonial uniform, he then only carried the revolver with him on his visits of the district outside of Kachanik. However, as the political department's boss in Skopje he always wore civilian clothing and always had a revolver and a 'knuckle duster' on him.

Our first house in Skopje was a rented house not too far from the CBD. Because dogs were not allowed in that rented house, Caesar had to be given away which upset us children very much. Caesar was our friend in many ways. In winter time he would pull us on the sled over the snow and in summer time he would play the retrieve-the-ball game with us.

One game I accidentally found that he liked to play in Kachanik was when I mischievously pushed him from the second storey window sill he liked to sit on watching the passers-by. What happened was he fell to the ground, landed safely and immediately ran up for some more of the 'game'. It was a miracle he was not only not hurt, but actually seemed to have liked it!

One of his tricks that we children liked very much was to come to our rescue when our father would punish us by belting us (hitting us with his belt) when we did something naughty. Caesar would sneak up behind my father, grab the belt from him and run away outside into the yard. That dog was loyal to us and although he got punished for doing it and told never to do it again, he never stopped. We were very grateful to him and as I said, we children were very upset when he had to be given away.

Two incidents involving Caesar after he was given away stand in my memory. First, several nights after Caesar had been re-homed, the neighbourhood was woken up with the loud sound of chains dragging on the street. This scared everyone as in those days only the jail inmates wore chains and everybody thought it was a jail break-out and the prisoners were on a killing spree seeking revenge. Needless to say, it was nothing like that, but Caesar who was strong enough to break the chains restraining him in the new place. Clearly, the new owner misjudged Caesar's strength by tying him only with ordinary chains to prevent him from escaping.

The second incident took place some months later. One day, we as a family were on an outing in the city park when this man on a bicycle, holding a cantering dog on a leash, came into sight. What happened next was something spectacular, to say the least. The dog was Caesar, who, on spotting us, immediately took off towards us with lightning speed, and as the man was still hanging on to the leash, rapidly accelerating the bicycle and the man on it at a terrifying rate. It was clear to everyone in that park, looking on at the proceedings, that there before their eyes was a really serious accident in the making. Luckily, the man quickly got over being stunned by the event, collected his wits about himself and let the leash go. However, the bicycle still continued rapidly over the grass and crashed into some flower beds. Caesar ran up to us and jumped all over us with joy (and dirty paws). We missed him for a long time.

On 23 September of the year we arrived in Skopje, my brother reached seven years of age, and this being the age proclaimed for starting school, he commenced attending a primary school located not too far from our home. As for me, for some reason still unknown to me, I had to wait not one and half years as expected by law before I could start school, but only six months. In fact, I started school immediately after we moved to another house, or rather a second storey unit, in a suburb in the hilly outskirts of Skopje that was much further from the CBD than our first house. The street name was 'Kiselovodska ulitsa', or the 'Mineral Water Street'. I guess, in the past there must have been a source of mineral water nearby.

Once again, I am not sure why we moved. It may have been dictated by my father's job, or it may have been associated with a change of air that the doctor said was required for medical reasons for my mother. Let me explain.

During the time we lived in the old house there was an epidemic of influenza in Europe and my mother caught it. I remember well how sick she was because she lost her voice and could not talk to us children and continually shoo-ed us away from her. We did not understand that she did this because she did not want us to catch the virus from her and instead thought that she was rejecting us. Also the doctor came almost every day and my father was home a lot which was not normal.

After several weeks my mother recovered from the influenza as such, but then she had to battle with some resultant complications. The influenza virus damaged her heart and her hearing. She could no longer do any strenuous work and even a slight physical exertion immediately caused her to run out of breath. She also became almost totally deaf and we had to speak very loudly, or actually yell, to communicate with her. Over the years, I have often thought how different my life may have been if penicillin had been available for my mother.

I also got very sick when we lived in the old house. I don't know what it was, the flu, diphtheria, malaria, or whatever, but I do remember it well, as my temperature was extreme and I was near death and delirious. I remember the feeling that I had of my lungs being squeezed and squeezed, tighter and tighter, as in a vice until they were almost bursting apart. Next, I had this most odd experience—I actually felt it—that I was falling and falling and falling into what seemed to be a bottomless pit. When I came to, I heard the doctor say to what seemed to be many people standing around the bed: 'The crisis seems over. I think he will live.' And that I did!

Interestingly, neither my father nor my brother got sick in the old house. Nevertheless, we moved, as I said, to this second storey unit in the outskirts of Skopje. If the reason for moving was to get fresher air then I am not so sure it was completely successful, because diagonally on the other side of the road from us was a soap factory and if the wind direction was right, we sure knew it was there!

As I recall it, our life in the unit was unexciting. Oh, yes. In these units we were allowed to have a house pet, so we got Nuli, a white poodle. He was no match to Caesar, but he was good company for my mother when my father was at work and we were at school and she was alone in the house. When somebody would knock at the door, Nuli would start barking and more importantly, run up to my mother excitedly, so she would know there was somebody at the door and go and see who it was.

With my mother being deaf and sickly it was a difficult time for all of us, but especially for her. My mother spent most of the time crocheting, reading, preparing meals and cooking cakes and jams—and we children always got to scrape the bowls which always had generous left-overs! Often there was a fight between me and my brother over who should get which bowl, namely the bigger cake mix bowl or the smaller, but the more delicious, icing bowl. Funny, how things like that are remembered!

Unlike in Kachanik, where gardeners, cooks and servants came with the government house, the houses where we lived in Skopje were not government but private and therefore our—and that means my father's—responsibility. In general, during our stay in Skopje, house cleaning, washing and ironing was done by a part-time cleaning lady and when she did not come, which was apparently her prerogative in those days of full employment, my mother had to do everything herself and we, of course, helped.

Because of her failing heart, which also affected her legs with elephantiasis, my mother was very weak and seldom left the unit, so we children had to run errands, like going to the corner shop and the nearest market. As my brother was quite shy, most of the time I had to actually go into the shop and ask for the item. When I was out playing with my friends and my brother had to go to the shop alone, he would stand outside the shop for some minutes, then come home and announce, 'They did not have it!'

In Skopje there was never the number of parties and people visiting us as was the case in Kachanik, even in the early days when my mother was her old healthy self, but after she got sick the frequency was even much further reduced. However, friends of the family still called in for something simple, like afternoon tea, and as we children eavesdropped on their meetings. Their talk was more and more often than not about Bolsheviks in the USSR, who by the definition of all White Russians the world over, were automatically no good, and about somebody called Hitler in Germany, who had these dangerous ideas of making all the people in the world his slaves—or something like that!

It was 1939/40 and as history tells us there was a lot of instability and sabre waving in Europe. Nations were readying themselves for a war. My father got busier and busier seeking out the 'fifth columnists', as persons sympathetic to external causes (Bolsheviks and Nazis in this case) who were bent on creating havoc in the country by blowing this or that up, were called. We children could sense that my father was concerned about the sort of things that were developing in the world, especially in our neck of the woods, and its effect on Yugoslavia and our safety.

Yugoslavia also was preparing for a conflict by doing military manoeuvres in various parts of the country and putting out 'information' leaflets—a euphemism for propaganda leaflets. Some of these leaflets were delivered to our place, and although my father thought they were unsuitable for children to read he did not destroy them. So, we read them. They were written in a simple enough language and had these scary cartoon-type drawings of the other side committing all sort of terrible acts and ghastly atrocities against the peace loving people of our side who would not even kill an ant in anger. In retrospect, and as will become clear later, I was too impressionable at that age and should not have read these leaflets.

As to the places where the military held manoeuvres, Skopje must have been thought an important enough place. I don't know if manoeuvres were the right description for what the military did, at least in Skopje, by having units of infantry, cavalry and armoured division march and trundle through Skopje with fanfare while the airforce planes were flying above in a show of strength. Some months later, when the German airforce bombed Skopje and the German army took less than half a day to conquer Skopje—and only ten days to conquer all of Yugoslavia—did I understand the difference between obsolete and modern.

Thus, the Yugoslavian force marching through Skopje with fanfare consisted of foot soldiers of the infantry, still in World War I-type outfit, complete with boots and bandaged calves, mounted unit of the cavalry with the man in the front proudly carrying a banner on a pole and some tanks of the armoured division that for some reason looked to me like tractors made up as tanks. The air force planes consisted of single engine biplanes of World War I vintage, flying at what to me, as an eight year old boy in a developing country as I mentioned before, was a super terrific speed of 90 km/hr!

In 1940/41 as part of the preparations for a war, training and information for the civilians commenced. This included storing tins of food and water, using gas masks, recognising the enemy planes, observing the blackout rule at night and preparing for air raids. The latter involved the officials sounding sirens that were installed in a number of locations around Skopje, with one very near our place. For us children it was a frightening experience to suddenly, without warning, when one least expects it, have this thing start up. My mother, of course, could not hear the siren and we had to indicate to her that the siren went off and we were supposed to go down to the basement.

In April 1941, as the sirens were still howling in what we were by then accustomed to be a training, we heard aeroplanes and then heard this ear piercing siren-like noise that far exceeded our usual siren sound, and then there was an explosion. As we hurried down to the basement, I glanced up at the window at the top of the stairs to momentarily see this thing with kinked wings, made of metal and not tarpaulin, as all the planes I had seen before were, hurtling down to the ground at a comet-like speed and about to crash. Of course, what I saw was a 'Stuka', the German dive bomber, that was designed, I am sure, not so much to inflict material damage to the other side, as to scare the daylight out of the civilians. And, actually, the result was just that: a bedlam, as people ran in panic to hide from it—and just about anywhere would do, it seemed!

The next day, or it may have been a few days later, I am not sure exactly, my father, who by now stayed at home, decided that it would be safer if we spent the day in the nearby hills and return home after it got dark and the planes could not attack. I remember, and so does my brother, that we spent the day in a cave as our base camp and as we children played outside clambering here and there over some ancient headstones and bits of other ruins of some sort, we found a gold coin. This is why we remember that episode so well, and also what happened on our way back home that evening.

At the end of the day as the darkness was setting in, we started walking home at a pace suitable for my mother. It was quite dark, but my father had a small battery torch that was enough to illuminate a bit of the road ahead of us, so we walked with safety. It was also very quiet except for our footsteps even though we were now passing houses on both sides of us. Then....suddenly in the darkness we saw some silhouettes, heard clicks of guns being readied and a gruff voice asking loudly, 'Who goes there?'—all, it seemed, happening at the one time.

On hearing the gun clicks and the voice, the pictures of the atrocities committed by the enemy I had seen in the 'information' booklets flashed through my mind and I instantly took off back towards the hills like a scared rabbit. As I took off I heard a gun being cocked and my father's voice: 'Don't shoot. It is my small son.' I ran in the darkness past the houses we had just passed and then I entered one of them—its door for some reason was not locked and yet nobody was inside—and hid under what later proved to be a large and solid dining room table.

I stayed under the table trembling with fear for what seemed to me to have been an eternity. A little later, I heard the voices of the owners in the next room; they must have returned from wherever it is they went to earlier. Then, a time later, I heard my father's voice in the next room asking the owners if they had seen a small boy anywhere here. At that instant I got out from under the table and ran into the room where my father and the other people were, ready to yell out, 'I am here!', but … as I remember it … no sound came out of my voice box.

When my voice did come back later, it did so with a stammer, which I had to endure for the next twenty years, or so. It was the most dreadful period of my life, especially when teased about it at school. It was cruel.

As only a true stammerer knows, the psychological effect is big and sometimes even extreme enough for the sufferer to commit suicide. I know. I was no exception. Stammering affected me very much, but … I managed to live with it and to conquer it in the end!

Returning to the incident, the silhouettes in the dark were nothing more sinister than the local gendarmes checking that people obeyed the blackout rule and making sure, as much as possible, that there were no thieves or other undesirables about. After I took off and my father explained who he was, namely the political inspector of the 'Banovina', the gendarmes saluted him and then continued their watch and my father, mother and brother went back up the hill well past the houses looking for me and then returned to knock at the door of every house. After I was found we all walked home and arrived there very late and exhausted.

In the next few days there were a few more air raids and there was a lot of commotion everywhere. People who were 'in the know', like my father, knew that the German invasion was imminent. He made preparations for it by getting his papers and documents in order, as well as, of course, stocking up on food for the family. Others seemed to sense that something bad was about to happen and there was then a run on shops as they, too, wanted to stock up on food, etc. It is tempting to describe this as 'a textbook case of panic buying', but to my mind it is not. The latter is a temporary effect because as soon as the goods are quickly re-supplied to the shops the buying returns to normal. But what happened in Skopje was not a temporary effect as it took something like fifteen years to get back to normality.

Next, it was only, I think, a matter of days before the German army 'blitzkrieg-ed' Skopje and then Yugoslavia. Here, I have made a verb of the German noun 'Blitzkrieg'. I have never done this before, nor have I ever seen anyone else do it, but to me this most succinctly describes what I saw actually take place. Let me explain further.

In German language 'Blitz' is a normal word, found in the dictionary, and it means 'lightning' and 'Krieg', also a normal word, means 'war'. In the German language, there are also many examples of normal words, i.e. concepts, obtained by combining two different words, to make a new concept. Although the resultant word is always longer, it is an efficient way of expressing a new concept and it also results in the economy of words. As far as I know, there has been no such word as 'Blitzkrieg' in the German language before World War II, for the simple reason that the concept it describes did not exist until then.

Thus, 'Blitzkrieg' describes the concept of a quick overwhelming of the enemy and a swift, simultaneous occupation of his country with the taking over of the control of its economy and its governance. I think it is now clear what the noun 'Blitzkrieg' means, and … all I have done is make a verb of it.

Because I noted above in connection with panic buying in Skopje that there it took fifteen years to get back to normality, I want to note here, too, rather than wait till later, that Skopje was also the last time I had a proper meal for a long time. In fact, the next time proper meals resumed for me was nine years later in Australia in 1949.

As the Germans took over Skopje they put into place their system of its governance. The blue print for this was to retain the existing basic administration departments and personnel and only have the top echelon supervised by an appropriate German person. This made sure that roads were repaired, garbage was collected, supplies were delivered, etc. In the case of the police, a similar system was practised except that more German personnel were at the top.

The above described take-overs by the Germans actually happened in Skopje, as a matter of German SOP (Standard Operating Procedure), if I can use this term. It is apt, though. However, because Bulgaria decided to put its money on the German side, the question of Macedonia cropped up. I don't know the history of Macedonia deeply enough to make definitive statements on behalf of any particular side, but I do know that Greece, Yugoslavia and Bulgaria, each claimed it to be theirs.

So, before the Turks occupied the region, Macedonia was with Greece and before the Germans occupied Yugoslavia, Macedonia was part of Yugoslavia. Now, it was the turn of the Bulgarians. It is that simple—at least in its essence—and so, the Germans handed over Macedonia to the Bulgarians.

In all of these goings on, I am not sure what the German SOP was for things like the local secret police and the 'Political Inspector's Section' with my father's not so envious position in it anymore. The fact was, of course, that he extricated himself. How, I don't know. He never talked about it. All I know, though, is that when the Bulgarians took over the administration of Macedonia, my father was declared a 'persona non-grata' and told to leave Macedonia fast—and we did. My poor mother!

CHAPTER III
The Tramping Year (1941)

We left Skopje for <u>Nish</u>,[1] a town in Serbia, where my father, who was still a government employee in the Public Service, with an official pay slip number, got a job in some administrative capacity there. His pay book was a very important document to have, even if pays were regularly late by a month, and more often by two months!

Father's paybook

Because we left Skopje in a hurry and because the railway service for household furniture was almost non-existent, we sold what we could and left behind or gave away, what we couldn't sell. We carried only the suitcases and soft bundles containing

---

1   I am really having a problem resisting writing the name of the town this way using four letters. In Serbian, either in Cyrillic or in Roman script, it is always a three letter word. (Ниш and Niš).

bedding, etc. My mother being sick and weak, my father and us boys had to carry and/or drag the suitcases and bundles; in Skopje from our second storey unit to the horse cart taking us to the station, then onto the railway platform there and then onto the train and then repeating these steps in reverse at the Nish end.

In Nish we rented a furnished unit—and not much furnishings either! As I remember, we all slept in the only one bed provided there—good thing it was a double bed! We slept like sardines: my father's and mother's heads at one end and us boys with our heads at their feet end.

Getting food was becoming a problem. Although ration coupons were introduced, they were often of no use as there was no stock in shops. Getting bread, the staple food in Yugoslavia— and for that matter in Europe—was a challenge, to say the least! The only way was to start queuing outside the bakery early in the morning to make sure you were reasonably near the door so that when the shop opened you would get in before the bread runs out. Initially, early in the morning meant about 6 am, then it became 5 am, 4 am, 3 am and so on.

Generally, my father would do the queuing, as our mother was too sick for that. What this meant was when my father was away for several days us boys had to it. I will tell you, experience like that makes you grow up really quickly and learn all the tricks of 'how to'.

Although we were supposed to be full time at school, for many reasons we were not. Much of our time was spent 'hunting' for food. My father was at work, but he took time off as often as it was possible and my mother was essentially an invalid for these kinds of practical purposes.

Often, when we were not successful in obtaining food—and here I must confess it sometimes included attempts at stealing the food—we either went hungry, or sold or bartered something for it. Clearly, there was a practical limit to how long one can continue doing this before nothing is left to sell or barter. At this point I want to comment in favour of the 'black market'.

Black market was prohibited by the Germans and anyone caught at it was punished—mildly at first in the beginning of their occupation of Yugoslavia (and in other countries, too), severely after a year or two and shot near the end, when the Germans were struggling to defend their positions against an advancing allied army.

To me, black market represents entrepreneurship; risky, of course, but so are all entrepreneurial activities. If we take a statistical view, we would find that the black market saved many more lives than were lost by the black market entrepreneurs, or the 'black marketeers'—a derogatory label used by the authorities—being shot. From my experience, during the time of near absolute austerity, when nothing of any practical use can be bought in shops, anything you need, or want, can be obtained on the black market—for a price, of course!

The opposite point of view, promulgated by the authorities, is that the black market is evil and it is it that caused the shortages in the shops in the first place. The logic of this position is that the removal of the black market from the market would immediately lead to goods being available in the shops for people to buy them whenever they want to. Now, then, really ... if you believe this you will believe anything, as they say. Experience has taught me that many an idea, absolutely faultless on paper, has a knack of either not working in practice at all, or working much less than was expected ideally.

Earlier I mentioned difficulties with getting bread our staple food and how we had to start queuing outside the bakery early in the mornings and so on. Let me now say a few words about the bread that I have had from 1941 till 1949, especially its colour, texture and taste.

I have eaten bread ranging in colour from bright yellow, through the various shades of brown, to jet black. There was never the white bread, not even much of it before the war; it was a luxury item. The yellow bread was the corn flour bread and the black one was the rye bread. The brown breads were the unrefined wheat flour breads. The textures ranged from smooth to coarse and lumpy. The former was due to mixing in of various kinds of grain, like sorghum, broken corn, rye and wheat, while the latter was due to adding diced potatoes to the 'dough'.

The bread that stands in my memory—and also in my taste buds—was the army bread. It was square shaped; it was never, ever fresh! Its colour was mid-brown; its texture was semi-rough; its taste was bland; its shelf life was pretty well indefinite; it contained all of the ingredients I mentioned above in connection with other breads, plus various amounts of munched straw, and its nutritional value was doubtful, except, perhaps, for horses, especially near the end of the war as its straw content increased!

But, back to Nish. It was becoming clear that we were experiencing hardship there. Sure, it being winter did not help, but even allowing for it the prognosis was not good. So my father thought that a move to Belgrade would make life easier, and in deciding this I think that he at last overcame his ego and accepted that being near my grandparents should be a help to us.

At this point I want to say that as long as I can first remember it, my father had this old-fashioned view, I guess, that in marrying my mother and taking her away from her parents' care, he accepted absolute responsibility for her and the resultant family after that, no matter what. It certainly never entered his mind before to ask for help or money from my grandparents. I know that they sent money and gifts to my mother and if my father found out about it, it made him very, very angry.

Two gifts that I remember my mother received from my

grandparents were a Singer hand operated sewing machine, and after she lost her hearing, an 'Aparatus Vibrafon', a Swiss-made, high-tech at that time, gadget, to help deaf people hear. It was a small, about 2 mm diameter and 5 cm long, corrugated silver tube, with a right angle kink in it at around its middle, with closed ends except for small openings in them. Unlike the hearing aids we are used to now, it was not battery operated, just a mechanical device that was supposed to magnify the sound vibrations. To use it, instructions said, simply insert one end into the ear, and point the other towards the front, so that people's voices will readily enter the open end.

How I remember my mother's excitement on receiving the gadget, packed in a beautiful looking box, as if it were a diamond broach. And how then I remember her disappointment when the thing had no significant effect at all. She tried just about everything she could think of, including writing to the agents/ manufacturers, but in the end it was put back in its box and the box put away in a wardrobe and abandoned. My poor mother. She suffered in silence—but we sensed it, and more so I than my brother. How come? Well, I had my own suffering to bear, namely the stammering. Remember?

¶

Thus, my father having decided to move to Belgrade after only about three months in Nish, we did not waste time and left Nish as the winter ended and spring was on its way. In Belgrade we rented a unit in Drinchicheva Street, which ended in the rather old Drinchicheva Markets. One benefit of being in this area of Belgrade was that it was not too far from the 'Professors Colony' where my grandparents lived.

The weather in Belgrade was getting warmer, so we had no

insurmountable problem keeping ourselves warm and clothed, but the food problem persisted. In connection with 'clothed', I remember that shoes and sandals were hard to come by, if not impossible. The reason was that the leather was required by the Germans for their war effort, soon to involve attacking and occupying the USSR. So, I made a pair of sandals from thick cardboard. It worked. I was able to walk in them quite well, but they wore out quickly because we walked everywhere in preference to catching a bus.

Remembering that we moved to Belgrade to be near my grandparents and their helping hand, in reality it turned out to be pretty well the opposite. The reason is explained below.

We know that Hitler and his cohorts were dead set at annihilating Jews and Gypsies, especially the Jews. This is well documented. But what seems to have been forgotten, or not known at all, is that they also had this thing about Masons. As it happened, my grandfather was a Mason and at that time, also its Grand Master. We didn't know that before and to hear that he was imprisoned because of it was a shock to us, especially, of course, to my mother. So, instead of the grandparents helping us, we had the job of comforting my grandmother who was alone in their house.

I must note here that I have been told later that the Germans referred to Masons as 'Judeo-Masons', meaning that Masons were in some way associated with Judaism. I am not competent to comment one way or other, but I do know that originally, Masons were a secret society. However, I believe this poster from the time exemplifies the sentiment. The text at the bottom reads: "Freemasonry is an international organization beholden to Jewry with the political goal of establishing Jewish domination through world-wide revolution." The map, decorated with Masonic symbols (temple, square, and apron), shows where revolutions took place in Europe from the French Revolution in 1789 through the German Revolution in 1919.

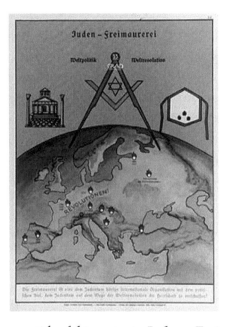

The German title of this poster is: **Juden – Freimaureri**
which translates: **Jews – Freemasons**

On arriving in Belgrade, my father went to see about a position in one of the public service departments, but I don't think he was overly successful. It seemed that there were more people than jobs in the public service at that time and my father's accent was no help. Although my father studied in a Yugoslavian university and graduated an LLD from it, he never became an accent-free speaker of the Serbo-Croatian language. On reflection, the same is true of me and the reason is the same, namely, by the time we started on the other language we were not as young and our voice boxes were then already permanently set to the original language.

One day, more or less two months after we arrived in Belgrade, my father announced that he has joined the army and that the family would be moving to Bela Crkva, pronounced Tsrkva—a small town in the province of Banat, where Yugoslavia adjoins Rumania (as the Slavic version of Romania is spelt) and also Hungary.

One can imagine the shock to my mother brought about by this announcement. But, as my father explained, there were no other practical options. The family needed the money to live on. My brother had to start high school. Belgrade was a big city where the cost of everything was high. My mother needed a quiet place where stress is low. Bela Crkva had a sizeable White Russian population and my father found out that my mother also had some school friends there, including one a doctor and another a dentist.

First, what's this: my father joining the army. Which army? The Germans were the occupying army and the Yugoslavian army was defeated with those who surrendered being sent off to POW camps. Those who did not surrender, but escaped to the mountains instead, vowed not to shave until they got the young King Peter II from England, to where he escaped when the Germans invaded his country, and restored him as the rightful ruler of Yugoslavia. These soldiers were led by the army general Drazha Mikhailovich and were known as 'Chetniks'. Needless to say that as the months went by and became years their hair and beards got to be pretty long indeed!

Then there were the communists in the same hills, too, led by Tito, a man who studied communism and its ways, including guerrilla warfare, in USSR.

Thus, we had the Germans, who ruled the country, the Chetniks who were against the Germans and fighting them the best they could and then there were the 'Titovtsi', that is, the communists led by Tito, who fought both the Germans and their own countrymen the Chetniks. It is a fact of history that the Allies were supplying both the Chetniks and the communist Titovtsi with arms and ammunition.

So, which army was my father joining? Well, a kind of a new army formed by the White Russians, who at last could see a chance of defeating, or at least help defeat, their old enemy the Bolsheviks, get back to Russia, restore the monarchy and live happily ever after. This army was fully backed by the Germans, of course! However, in the back of their mind the Germans had a different idea to what they led the White Russians believe as to what function this army would have.

As it transpired later, the Germans saw this army, which was called the 'Schutzkor', or the 'Security/Guard Corps' as taking over the domestic guard duties and fighting Titovtsi and Chetniks, and so freeing the German soldiers for the East and the West fronts. Now, the 'Schutzkort-si', fighting the former, that is, the communists was no problem as they were the traditional enemy, but. ... Chetniks were the royalists, just like the Schutzkort-si, were in the Tsar's Russia in 1917 and this did not gel well.

The fact that the Schutzkor soldiers, that is my father and the other White Russians, wore the Wermacht—the German Army uniform—with only an arm band differentiating them, was not helpful in winning friends among the local population. However, in the initial enthusiasm of having an army of their own, which they believed would fight the Bolsheviks in the Soviet Union, the White Russians either did not know of what the Germans really had in mind, or did not want to see the obvious or think about it. After all, the name 'Schutzkor' was a dead give-away! Then again, in the nature of things the White Russian Schutzkor soldiers were by now mostly in their late forties and fifties, so they were more akin to 'Dad's Army' of the TV series fame, than young, virile soldiers suitable for the Eastern Front.

I say the above from experience which included personally

spending six weeks of my 1942 school holidays with my father's regiment in Pozharevats, a town some 100 km from Belgrade. And ... yes, you've guessed it—a cavalry regiment! I had a ball, as they say. Playing with other children in the haystacks, fetching things for grooming the horses, helping groom them, learning how to saddle a horse, tie a rope properly and a few times actually accompanying the unit on its routine inspection of the nearby country side. It was OK, I guess, and it was experience, but I don't think I was suitable for this sort of recreation as each time I ended up with a very sore bottom!

So, there were some misgivings being in a German-backed army. However, at that time in Yugoslavia, being in a German-backed army of any kind had some pretty important advantages; the main one of them all was food—glorious food! If you were in the army you got fed, clothed and medically treated when sick. Also, your family received your pay. Need I say more! Remember Darwin? Survival of the species is the strongest force on earth.

CHAPTER IV

The Bela Crkva Years (1941 - 1944)

Back to the family moving from Belgrade to Bela Crkva. As I said, Bela Crkva was a small town with a population of about 8,000 consisting of sizeable proportion of White Russians, German settlers, known as 'Volksdeutch' and Hungarians—the rest being Yugoslavs. Strangely, there were hardly any Rumanians, yet Rumania is no more than 20 km away. The White Russians had built quite an infrastructure in Bela Crkva. There was, of course, the church, the library, the girls' school of the kind that my mother went to when she was young and the boys' military school that my brother and I went to.

Bela Crkva means 'White Church' and, in fact, on approaching the town the first building you see is a white church, before any other buildings come into view. When we moved there its name was officially 'Weisskirchen', which is the German for 'White Church'. In fact, many places in Yugoslavia had different names during the German occupation—with the names being mainly 'germanised'. An example close to us is Novi Sad. It was 'Uividek', which means 'New something' in Hungarian, when it was part of the Austro-Hungarian Empire, then Novi Sad, or 'New Sad', under Yugoslavia and then it was changed to 'Neusatz', meaning 'New Satz', when the Germans came and then back to Novi Sad when the Red Army 'liberated' Yugoslavia in 1945. It is still Novi Sad as I write this (2013).

So, we moved to Bela Crkva. There we rented a two bedroom extension to a house— something like a 'granny flat' we have in

Australia—owned by a Colonel Potapov. He was an ex White Russian Army colonel who in Bela Crkva was a teacher of Russian history in the 'Russkii Kadetskii Korpus', a military type high school in the old Russian mould that my brother and I attended. For simplicity let me from now on call it the 'Cadet School'. My father moved us in and several days later he left to rejoin his army unit. But before he left, he enrolled my brother in the Cadet School and me in the Primary School a couple of blocks away for my final (4th) year, before I, too, would enter the Cadet School in September 1942. He also organised a small 'get together' of my mother's school friends in the house, so we boys could get to know them if help for my mother was needed urgently. It was more important for me to get to know them than it was for my brother, because I, a ten year old boy, was to take the major part in looking after my sick mother and liaising with her friends. This is because, as will be seen later, entering the Cadet School, meant boarding there as well, even though the school was within a walking distance from our home in Bela Crkva. I know this may sound crazy, to say the least, but rules were rules—and that's all that was to it!

So, I was left with my mother, and most of the time when I was not in school, I helped by putting on the best performance I could. Although I was still ten years old, I did try to act older. I did run messages, like going to the shop to buy this or that, go to fetch the doctor when my mother was in a bad way and then go to the chemist to get the prescription filled—and that was an experience and half. Unlike nowadays, when getting a prescription filled is no more cleverer than sticking the computer generated label onto a bottle, tube or a box of the ready made medicine, the old ways of filling a prescription was an art as well as a science. Powder and stuff had to be weighed on an analytical-type balance, put in a pestle and mortar and really worked on by hand, adding drops of liquid, if a paste was required; then an appropriate glass jar—there were no plastic jars then—was chosen and the contents scraped into it with a spatula. The label was written by hand and glued on with an adhesive paste freshly made that day. Filling a liquid mixture prescription was even more of a performance, requiring deft hands; 'superb' would be an appropriate description.

On some days a cleaning lady would come and that was a great help to my mother who was house proud and would try to do it herself. So, my mother and I just continued with our daily routines and we got on together famously. I helped her and she helped me and comforted me, especially with bad earaches that I suffered with as a child. There were no sulpha drugs then! She used to heat some camphor oil in a spoon and pour it into my ear and then wrap a hot brick in a towel and I held that against my ear. Primitive, yes, but what were the alternatives? None really.

Although I did try to act older as I noted above, after all is said and done I was still a ten year old boy, and Colonel Potapov was an enthusiastic fisherman and like all fishermen the world over, he liked to gloat about his catches and about 'the one that got away'. Well, it was a forgone conclusion that I would catch his enthusiasm for fishing. Where did people fish in Bela Crkva? Sure, Danube was not prohibitively far away—just under an hour, or so in a car. But we did not have a bicycle, or a horse, let alone a car, so the fishing place had to be within a reasonable walking distance. And amazingly, there it was, some 10–15 minutes away by foot—an old quarry filled with water and fish! I guess, if you didn't know, or look too carefully at it, you might think it was a small natural lake.

I must admit, I liked fishing in that place, or rather watching the cork attentively and hoping it would suddenly go under … and sometimes it did! Well, I got hooked on fishing, so to say, and many a time I skipped school just to go fishing. I was quite naughty and took advantage of my mother being sick and not able to visit the school to check, by telling her fibs that, 'It was a good day at school. I had great time and learned a lot'. One day, I almost did not return home. I got too close to the edge, the earth gave way under me and I ended in the water drowning as I could not swim. I wondered then if I was being punished for lying to my sick mother? Luckily for me, a man was passing by at about the same time, saw what happened and pulled me out.

The other recreational activity I was hooked on in Bela Crkva was reading books. As I noted earlier, there was a Russian library in town and I discovered they had all of the Connan Doyle stories of the exploits of Sherlock Holmes, in Russian, of course! Well, I often read these stories late into the night, by candle light! until I got to the end of the book. I simply couldn't stop before then.

Then, too, I liked going to the movies, but I was not really hooked on them. For a starter, they were all silent movies, with a wind up gramophone on a table below the screen providing scratchy music. And then, the movie theatre, well … actually an old assembly hall of some sort, was airless and smoky—smoking being allowed in disregard of any fire safety rules, that is, if there were any!

So, life went on for me and my mother. Luckily, there was enough food around, nothing fancy, mind you, but wholesome enough. There were a few villages nearby where fresh vegetables and eggs could be purchased. So, as regards food, it was much better in Bela Crkva than it ever was in Nish or Belgrade. On some special days my brother would come to spend the day with us and once that year my father came on his two week vacation from the army.

Talking about eggs reminds me how we got a hen and put her in the small yard we had at the back to wait for the eggs she was supposed to lay. To make the hen happy, I made a necklace by stringing some corn together and put the necklace on her neck. The next morning the hen was found dead. She had apparently tried to eat the corn and in the process strangled herself. Stupid hen!

In June 1942, I finished primary school, and as I was already enrolled in the Cadet School to start in September of that year, I went to spend six weeks of my summer holidays with my father in his cavalry unit in Pozharevats, as I have already mentioned before. My brother stayed in Bela Crkva to be with our mother.

After coming back to Bela Crkva from my holidays it was not that long before I, too, entered the Cadet School. Let me tell you about the Cadet School and, as it dominated our lives for the rest of our stay in Bela Crkva, I go in to some detail.

For some one hundred and fifty years before the 1917 Revolution the Imperial Russia had a number of the so called 'Kadetskii Korpus', or Cadet Schools. These schools were essentially a military academy for high school students. Noting that the primary school was a four year study program and a high school, or 'gymnasium', to give it the European name, was an eight year one, the 'recruits' to these Cadet Schools were the 10–11 year old boys who had finished primary school and were about to enter a 'gymnasium'. The Imperial Russian Army had its future officers recruited largely from the graduates of these schools and most, but not all, boys entering these Cadet Schools had it in mind to follow a military career after graduation.

Me as a cadet

The routine in these Cadet Schools was absolutely military. Everything was done by the bugle, from waking you up in the morning to putting you to bed at night. The cadets lived in barracks and discipline was the order of the day. They wore the Imperial Russian Army uniforms, as can be seen in the photo of me in the uniform when I started my first year in the Cadet School. This photo documents me as a cadet in a close-up. Later on there is a group photograph of the cadets in the same uniform and the same cap, but I cannot be seen distinctly there.

What cannot be seen under the cap in the photo is the bald head. As I noted earlier, we always had our hair cut short, or rather shorn. The idea was to prevent head lice and if you got them, then it is much easier to find and squash them if there is no hair!

In the Cadet School all the activities—and everything else, too, it seemed—was regimented; attending classes, having meals, doing sport, doing gardening duties, attending church services, having medical check-ups, preparing for the annual show, doing drills and parades—and they were never ending!; marching into town to attend civic ceremonies, marching to the cemetery for funeral services, and so on.

There was a definite pecking order, or to give it the official name, the order of saluting officers, seniors, unit leaders and those who had a pip or two on their epaulettes.

The eight years were divided into three groups, or 'rota' to give it the Russian name. Years one and two were the Group III, years three to six were the Group II and years seven and eight were the Group I. So, imagine if you just started, like when I did, and you happen to be walking and passing all these people, even if they were on the other side of the street, the amount of saluting that had to be done; up to your cap and down again, up to your cap and down again, and so on … was enough to make your arm want to fall off! And, look out if the salute was even a tinsy-winsy bit out of standard; back in the barracks you are in for a saluting session of one hour or more. Then your arm just about will fall off and not just want to fall off! And, of course, before you were allowed to go into town, you had to have a very good reason and have your uniform inspected with a fine comb and nail brush.

The Cadet School in Bela Crkva started in the town of Sarajevo in Bosnia and was moved to Bela Crkva a few years before the war began. Its full name was 'Pervyi Russkii Kadetski Korpus Velikogo Knyaza Konstantina Konstatinovitcha'—and what a mouthful it is! A translation is no shorter either, namely: 'First Russian Cadet School Named After The Grand Duke Konstantin Konstatinovitch'.

Actually, the Cadet School did not start in Sarajevo, but was transferred there from Russia where it was the first cadet school named after the said Grand Duke in the country. Its existence in Yugoslavia got the blessing and the support of King Alexander I, the assassinated father of the boy King Peter II, who you will remember escaped to England with his uncle Duke Paul who was carrying the state's gold, it was said, when the Germans occupied Yugoslavia. The reason King Alexander I supported the school was because he was educated in the Imperial Russia in one of these cadet schools and, I guess, must have liked the experience. But then he was royalty, wasn't he? And so would have been at the top of the saluting list, not so?

When my brother started the Cadet School in Bela Crkva, the school was located in the outskirts of the town in a massive three storey stone barracks. The building was really impressive with long corridors and many rooms and dormitories. One of the large rooms was the museum containing the sacred icon—the school's historic banner that we were taught to guard with our lives as it must never fall into the enemy hands—and all kind of assorted military paraphernalia.

The whole thing stood on a large piece of land, part of which was the assembly square/parade grounds and the remainder— cultivated. It's no wonder that the Germans commandeered it for their troops and the school had to move to the not so large buildings of the girls' school at the other end of town. I really don't know what happened to the girls and their education. I guess, somebody knows, including some of the girls who could still be alive somewhere.

When I started in September 1942, the Group III cadets, that is, previous year's intake and us, the raw recruits or 'the rookies', were dormitored in a large single storey house, about five houses away from the main two storey barracks. Each unit had an officer-in-charge. Ours was Captain Hartonov, the only captain in the School; the others were all colonels and, of course, the Cadet School Commander was a general, in our case Major-General Popov, or 'GenPop' as we called him amongst ourselves.

Captain Hartonov had lost one arm in the war, so he only had one good arm and a stump just below his shoulder where the other arm should have been. But don't think he was an invalid. Far from it! He was as strong as an ox. One common punishment meted out to cadets for minor misdemeanours was for an officer, or a senior to give you a 'schekoldyshka'. I don't think it is translatable into English. A schekoldyshka entailed its giver holding your head under his arm and with the other hand clenched, rolling his knuckles over your head. It hurt like blazes. Remember our heads were always shorn hairless! Captain Hartonov's 'schekoldyshka' was acknowledged by all cadets to hurt the most while his stump held your head like a vice!

The other common punishment meted out to cadets for minor misdemeanours was 'parasha' and then usually in multiples. In English parasha means a 'night can'. So, to be punished with, say, 'three parashas', meant that for three mornings you had to take the night can from the dormitory, housing some 25–30 boys, to the toilet—actually a hole in the ground in a one man shed in the back yard of the house—and empty it, there being no such service provided by the town council. As far as I recall, no cadet escaped this punishment and some had it many times. In fact, this makes sense when you think about it. For hygienic reasons the can had to be emptied every day and if we did not have to do it, who would have had to do it? Not the officers, that's for sure! So, even if we behaved like angels some fault would have needed to be found to give us 'N parashas' where N stands for the actual number of cans requiring emptying. There would be no point in giving a punishment that exceeded this number!

Whilst the subject is punishment, that given for major misdemeanours ranged from standing at attention near a wall, or as we called it 'supporting the wall', for anything from one hour to a whole day, to being expelled. And look out if the officer or a senior caught you standing at ease 'supporting the wall'. The punishment time was immediately doubled! Yes, a cadet's life was tough. It was so on purpose. It was meant to be tough. You either survive, or you don't. And if you don't, then you leave and in the end only the best are left behind—a kind of natural selection, one might say.

A typical day for us was up with the bugle in the morning, then ablutions and inspection. This consisted of the unit standing two deep at attention. The duty cadet, a different one each day according to the roster, had to beforehand check for anything unusual that may have happened overnight and count the heads. Then he would stand at the top of the line and wait for the unit officer, in our case Captain Hartonov, to ceremoniously appear and stand in front of the unit at attention—the unit was standing at attention, not the officer! Next, the duty cadet would march the few steps up to the officer, salute him and make his report.

Oh, how I hated this reporting duty when it was my turn! I dreaded it. It made me sick for days beforehand. I would march up to the officer and salute, and click my heels again and again, to coax the report to come out my mouth. The initial few seconds silence was most embarrassing as I could see the cadets, especially those in the back row, laugh secretively. Then, when the words came out it was with a heavy stutter. I would have given anything to have one of my friends do the reporting part for me, but it was not allowed by the School Rules. It was cruel. Oh, God how I wished I was dead!

After the assembly and reporting, we would do the morning exercises and then, when the bugle announced it, we would march to the main building for breakfast in the dining hall, which once or twice a year, doubled as an indoor assembly hall for speeches and presentations, gymnastics hall, a theatre and a ballroom.

Usually, all the three Groups were present and each would march in and stand at the chair at which he happened to come to as part of the line. Then the school commandant, General Popov, the other officers and the school chaplain would walk in and stand at the head table. On each table there was a tray of cut bread, one slice for each person. Whilst all this officers' ritual was going on, each one of us would scan the table to see where the 'gorbushkas' were, namely the end slices of the bread, which, because of its French shape, were always slightly bigger than the thinner slices in between.

Next, we would sing the appropriate hymn followed by the school chaplain saying the grace. Then, on the command 'Sit' many hands would simultaneously shoot out towards the nearest gorbushka. I can tell you that at times like this it was a distinct advantage to have long arms!

After a set time for eating, the procedure, sans the gorbushka bit, would be reversed: on the command 'Stand' we would stand

and sing the thanks grace, the chaplain would say it, the officers would leave, the command 'March' would be given and we
would march out into the assembly square. There we were able
to mingle together until the bugle announced the next activity,
which on school days was lessons as per appropriate time table.

The same routine as for breakfast would be repeated for lunch
and dinner, except that the quantities of food were different, the
breakfast and dinner being the smallest, as per the Continental
practice. Needless to say, as growing boys, we needed more food
than was provided, so we always looked forward to the (food)
parcels from home.

After dinner, there was usually time allotted for doing homework set by the teacher of this or that subject. Then, it was the
bugle to bed and lights out. As per standing orders, there was
always a cadet on night watch duty. This practice seems to be
typically Russian as these night watch duty persons can be found
in practically every building in Russia, including in all hotels, and
then on each floor!—as every tourist and visitor knows.

On weekends, or rather Sundays, because Saturdays were
working days, there would be a church service in the main building. Of course, we would all march there and stand close together,
right through the service, which in Russian Orthodox practice
never takes less than two hours. We stood close together, not
for support, though God knew we could do with it, but because
it was a small church, or more accurately, a big room inside the
main school building fitted out as a church.

Talking of the main building, it is surprising what it had
inside. Apart from the church I have just mentioned, there was
also a small, 5 or 6 bed mini-hospital, or 'lazaret', as its official
name was, with a full-time male 'feldsher' in charge—a kind of
semi-doctor— and a nurse, or maybe two.. A proper doctor, and
a dentist, both my mother's old class mates from the girls school,

used to visit regularly, or attend an emergency when called by the feldsher because the injury was outside his knowledge or experience. Then, there was the museum on the second floor, not as big as the museum in the old barracks that were now occupied by the German soldiers, but it seemed to hold—just!—all of the paraphernalia from the old museum.

As my family knows, the main building is now a 'Kategoria D' hotel. Not category B, or even C, but D, mind you! How many stars is that? One, a half? What a let down from its heydays as the Cadet School! Sure, there are no bathrooms and toilets in the rooms. But there is a communal one on the second floor, as it was in our time there. And sure, the water supply was capricious and hot water, well ... you did get it sometimes—it is not that it did not exist or that you never got it. So what's wrong with that? No, I just think the modern tourists are too spoiled for their own good!

¶

It was during an otherwise normal day at school when I learned of my mother's death. I was in a classroom attending a lesson, I am almost sure it was religion because when I was called out of the classroom to be told that my mother had died, the priest seemed to have appeared almost instantly to comfort me. My brother was in the main building, attending lessons in another subject, and he, too, was called out to be told the sad news. Then we both walked home to find a number of people there and my mother being laid out on a special stand by the undertakers, as required by the orthodox religion that the deceased's face be uncovered. Yes, we cried. A lot. Our eyes were red. We were comforted by my mother's friends. As the night came we couldn't sleep. Although there were few other people in the house, we couldn't stop thinking of our mother in the next room.

Mother's death certificate, written in German language

Of course, my father had been notified, but his army unit was on manoeuvres, or something, and, as we found out later, he did not get the message immediately, but only two days later.

Because there were no proper morgue facilities in Bela Crkva at that time, the funeral had to be carried out the next day and everybody hoped that my father had received the message and would make it. But, of course, he did not receive the message until it was too late.

My mother's funeral was a very sad experience for me. I was deeply moved saying good bye to her according to the Russian Orthodox custom, by kissing her cold, motionless, face. She looked serene and in peace. I suppose she was happy, too, because the pain and suffering has stopped. She used to take valerian mixture for a long time, then morphine—and much of it near the end. Then I vividly remember walking, sombrely, with my head bent down, behind the horse-drawn hearse to the cemetery and there seeing the coffin slowly descend into the grave, and the grave then be covered with earth. So, that was it! The sad end of one chapter of my life.

The missing mourners were, of course my father, and also my grandparents. As I noted elsewhere, my grandfather was in a Belgrade jail for being a Mason and I suppose my grandmother was too upset, and sick with worry, to make it to the funeral. Besides, travel from one place to another in those difficult times was not your piece of cake it now is, so, I guess, she thought the better of it and did not come. In fact, the last time I saw my grandmother was the year before in 1941 and then never again.

When finally my father arrived a few days after the funeral, we, that is he, me and my brother, went up to the cemetery which is on the hill overlooking a large part of Bela Crkva.

Later—I remember it well—we sat in the park and talked. I can't remember it all, but I do recall us talking about a headstone for the grave because it was a strong custom to have one, and the only thing that has to be decided is whether to have the deceased's photo on it, or not. I can't recall the latter part, but I recall we agreed to have a headstone made as soon as my father could organise it.

In the event, no headstone was organised before we left Yugoslavia and, in fact, it had to wait another 30 years before it was done. Following the death of my father in 1970 in Australia, to where we migrated in 1949, I decided to visit Yugoslavia and went to Bela Crkva to organise a headstone for my mother's grave. The photo shows the finished headstone with the inscription that it was erected by my brother and I in Australia, in loving memory of our mother.

Three years later I returned, with my children Tanya and Peter in tow, to formally bless the headstone by the priest and say special prayers for her soul, as required by the Orthodox Church. Also visiting the grave at this time was Mrs Semenova, to be mentioned later as the lady who helped organise the building of the grave and the headstone.

At Mother's grave blessing ceremony

Mother's grave

Other thing I remember my father telling us, as we sat on the bench in that park, was that now we are on our own and will no longer have, or need, a house. From now on we will continue to stay in the Cadet School and whenever it is possible spend our summer vacations with him, that is, if his battalion is still in Yugoslavia.

The next day my father arranged for whatever furniture we had to be sold and our personal memorabilia to be stored in the attic of the house owned by my mother's class mate, Mrs Rumjantseva—also Natasha. They owned a house, in the same street and not too far from the Potapov's where we lived. She was a dentist and her husband, Volodya, was a dental mechanic. My brother and I always called them Aunt Natasha and Uncle Volodja. Being the only dentist in Bela Crkva, they were well off and always had enough food which was brought in by the patients from the nearby villages as payment for their dental treatment.

The Rumjantsevs had a daughter, Lena, my age and I sometimes went to their house to play games with her. Frankly, she was a spoiled child and always argued with me about who won this or that game, etc. I did not like her all that much. I was to come and live with them for a few weeks two years later, but … that's later.

¶

After my mother's funeral and my father's visit and disposing of all our possessions, we were virtually left in what we stood. But then, we had the cadet uniforms: summer, winter and ceremonial ones. Summer and winter uniforms could also be called, correspondingly, light and heavy. They were both same colour, namely, green, but the winter uniform was made of a heavier cloth and came with a grey coat. The ceremonial uniform included a white shirt. As to the socks and boots to go with the uniforms, well … it's like this: there were never socks and never shoes as part of the uniform. Yes, that's a fact and an experience in its own right! I am sure it must be documented somewhere in history—and if not, then it ought to be—that for years, if not for centuries, the Imperial Russian Army marched in 'partyanki', that is, rectangular pieces of thick cotton. Once you have mastered putting them on your feet, so many blisters later, they were comfortable enough and/or you got used to them.

There were many advantages of partyanki. For a start, there was no left and right one and no foot size—all partyanki fitted all feet, no matter what size or shape. They were easy to wash and to mend, that is if anybody bothered to mend one. Actually, if a hole appeared, you simply twisted the rectangle of the partyanki, so that the part with the hole in it would now be covered by a solid fold as you wrapped the thing round your foot. It's a breeze—if you are an origami expert!

Now the boots. In connection with our stay in Belgrade I did note earlier that I made a pair of sandals out of thick cardboard because of a lack of leather in the country. So, when all the leather-sole boots that the school had in the store wore out, wooden sole boots, still with leather uppers—and not uppers made out of thick tent material—were introduced. They were awful and a real pain to walk in. I don't know how the Dutch do it with their clogs—or is it just a gimmick to promote tourism?

Really, if you examine the anatomy of a foot and the physics of walking, you would see that there has to be a bending of the toes, or rather the front part of the foot. If not, there is no fulcrum action as required by the physics and the feet move not only clumsily, but unsafely also. Luckily, somebody patented a wooden sole with a hinge there, so we had that later and it was great—still with clomp, clomp, clomp, but less noisy. Incidentally, somebody else thought of a wooden sole with multiple hinges and that proved a real boon for sandals.

So, time went by for us in Bela Crkva, each day being kind of routine.

The summer 1943 vacation, that is, the months of July and August, my brother and I spent in a youth hostel in the outskirts of Belgrade, in the diametrically opposite direction to where my grandparents' house was. So, there was no easy way we could go to visit them. Also, it would have been pretty pointless, as my grandfather was still in prison and my grandmother was being looked after by a day lady.

On returning to Bela Crkva, life resumed again from where we left it before we went for holidays.

My brother was now in year 3 and that meant he was in Group II in the main building.

I was in year 2 and therefore still in Group III in the nearby house I referred to before.

That year nothing extraordinary happened, as I recall it, except perhaps for my losing the platinum cross that hung round my neck since I was a little boy. It was given to me as a blessing, but by whom, I don't rightly know. My brother had one also, but his was gold. So, losing something like that cannot be forgotten.

I know exactly where I lost the cross and the circumstances surrounding the loss. Outside the main school building there was a park and the cadets used to play there during their free periods. Well, one day at the end of one of those activities, I noticed that my cross had gone. It must have happened during a rather boisterous contact with a classmate. I looked for it then and again on several days afterwards, but the grass was long and it was nowhere to be found.

As the year marched on, there was a perceptible and continuous change in the air, so to speak. Thus, some food was getting scarcer, people were talking more softly in groups, we had to forgo the school's usually big Christmas tree party and generally tighten our belts. What was happening, of course, is that the German Army defeats here and there had repercussions back in their occupied countries.

There were also more attacks against the Germans by both the royalist 'Chetniks' and the communist 'Titovtsi', or guerillas as they were collectively called, as they got more courageous as the Germans' defeats elsewhere increased.

The outcome of these increased attacks by the guerrillas, was that the Germans issued an edict, namely: 'For every German soldier killed there will be 50 detainees executed and for every German officer killed 100 detainees will be executed'. The detainees were the local residents detained in camps and jails on such crimes as being suspected of being sympathetic to guerrillas, as well as all sort of other 'hard' and 'soft' criminals. I guess my grandfather was included and whether he was in a 'hard' or 'soft' category was really immaterial.

And yes, there were these executions. And yes, by both a firing squad and by hanging. The former you could hear and the latter you could see for yourself afterwards. I remember going by train and seeing bodies, and not only of men, hanging from every telegraph post for quite some distance along the way. Not a pretty sight. But … that's how wars are.

Anyway, soon the 1943/44 end-of-year examinations started and we were all focussed on studying hard for these. Incidentally, the end-of-year referred to above, means the school year not the actual year, that is, September to June. That year, my second year in the cadet school, I did reasonably well in my exams, as can be seen from my exam results, and I received a Certificate of Merit.

As was the Cadet School practice, cadets who did well in exams earned a pip on their epaulettes and I was looking forward to the start of the new school year in September, so I could wear the uniform with a pip and make many of my classmates and others, who tormented me, jealous with envy—and, best of all, to salute me when required!

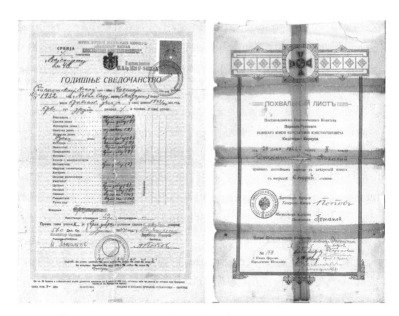

(Left) Year 2 exam certificate, (Right) Year 2 merit certificate

However, before the pip and all that, there was the summer vacation to get through. That year we were to spend it with our father in Smederevo—an industrial town on the Danube—where his unit, now without horses, was on guard duty of an oil refinery. So, my brother and I got on the train in Bela Crkva and eventually found our way to Smederevo where our father met us and installed us in a rented one bedroom unit in the outskirts on the other side of the town and away from all the industry—and just as well!, because some days later, at night, the allied planes bombed that part of town targeting the refinery, of course.

I remember as my brother and I watched the proceedings and seeing the effect of the bombing, namely a huge fire illuminating the countryside like a giant torch, allowing us to see each other very clearly, yet we were, I guess, some 10–12 km away from the fire. We could also see the many searchlight beams directed towards the sky, and a plane, or two, caught in the beam and glistening ever so brightly. We could also hear the anti-aircraft guns firing incessantly at the planes and we saw one plane being hit. It started to plummet immediately as a fire ball—all very spectacular. I hope the men in the plane were able to jump out of it before it got to the fireball stage. Because of it being night time we could not see clearly whether there was anybody parachuting down or not.

As it happened, it was the first bombing raid on Smederevo—just our luck! Incidentally, at that stage of the war all Allied bombing raids were carried out at night time, because it is a matter of the war records that the earlier day time bombing raids resulted in unacceptable casualties of the Allied planes. It also looked like the refinery was hit. We knew that because we could see the oil flames going up, but, of course, we did not know whether the guardhouses were hit and particularly the one that our father was in.

The refinery was situated on a piece of land adjoining the river Danube. The refinery had its own harbour where some tankers bringing in the crude oil and other tankers taking the refined gasoline out, would dock, essentially side by side. On each corner of the refinery there stood a guardhouse—a pretty solid piece of thick reinforced concrete with heavy metal doors, small windows and a flat roof with machine guns on it. It housed about 10–12 guards and had sleeping bunks, a kitchen with cooking facilities, a store for provisions, an ammunition store and a mess with table and chairs. I know all that, because my brother and I spent a few single days there with our father and the other guards. In the evenings, before it got dark, we would return to our one bedroom unit on the other side of town.

At about lunch time the next day after the bombing raid, we got the news that although his guardhouse was hit by a bomb, there were no casualties and our father was OK. In fact, the following day he was able to come to our unit and take us with him back to the refinery. What we saw was quite amazing. There were deep craters near the guardhouse where the bombs exploded and a sizeable crack on the sidewall of the guardhouse running from the ground level up to the flat roof and little in along the roof. I guess, if the crack ran all the way along the roof and down again on the other side, the whole structure may have cracked open like a nut. But everything was OK and there was no need to evacuate the guardhouse, so it just continued to stand there 'on guard', so to speak.

On another occasion, I remember, the bombing raid was not lucky for one Allied plane and its crew, as for some reason the plane came down in the river and the blackened bodies were washed ashore for everybody, including us boys, to see in the morning. Incidentally, the next time we saw blackened bodies in the same river, they were of German soldiers … but that's later.

These bombing raids were not all negative events for the people down on the ground; there was often also one benefit: stunned fish in the bomb craters on the river shores—but you had to be quick! Remember, food was scarce then.

Talking about refinery, oil and bombing raids, reminds me that I forgot to mention that a few weeks before we left Bela Crkva for Smederevo, there was a huge glow one night over the southeast Rumania that we could see in Bela Crkva. We were told it was a bombing raid on the Ploeshti oil fields that fully destroyed the oil production there.

The destruction of the Ploeshti oil fields in Rumania and the bombing of the refinery in Smederevo had a big effect on the German war effort—and it almost cost me my life! … but that's later, again.

When we were not with our father in his 'fortress guardhouse' in the refinery, we used to occupy ourselves by playing all manner of games with the local children, going on outings to nearby fields and forests and other tourist areas in Smederevo.

One of these 'tourists sights' was the steelworks named SAR-DID. Translated, it stands for Serbian Mining and Metallurgical Company Proprietary Limited and it still exists to this day (2015), but with a more responsible care for the environment. At the time we were there it was the biggest steelworks in Yugoslavia and I suspect, almost certainly the dirtiest! What, with antiquated charging of iron ore and coke into antiquated blast furnaces and then refining the molten pig iron in Bessemer converters, with just a token hood over them to catch the smoke billowing from them, certainly resulted in lots of pollution.

Seeing all that dirt, made me vow then and there that I will never ever be involved with ironmaking and their blast furnaces and will always stay away as far as possible from anything that remotely had to do with it. Really?? How come then that I became a metallurgist with an international reputation in blast furnaces? Good question … but that's much, much later, still.

One activity we liked in Smederevo during our stay there was swimming in a nearby pond. It was summer and very hot and humid, so swimming was a refreshing past time. We did this as often as possible even though the water in the pond was not the freshest. There was a footbridge over the narrowest part of the pond and we enjoyed jumping from it. To this day I wonder how as many boys survive to become men as they do—all the stupid and dangerous things boys do, to mainly show off to their peers. The kind of 'See how good I am. I dare you to do the same,' mentality.

Well, a few days before my brother and I were due to leave Smederevo to get back to Bela Crkva for the start of the school year, I either got bitten just above my right knee by some creature living in the pond, or I hit something odd while doing those crazy jumps from the bridge. Irrespective of what, or how it actually happened, there was this swelling starting above my right knee, that in few days got so big that it enveloped my knee as well. What rotten luck! Just as we had to depart for Bela Crkva. Of course, there was no question of postponing the return journey. So, off we went by train, my brother and I, not as able bodied for such a venture as should normally be the case. In retrospect, I should have had crutches. It would have made me so much faster and moving about would have been less painful as well. But, here I was hobbling along behind my brother.

We got on the train in Smederevo and eventually arrived in Belgrade's main railway station expecting to change there, more or less on arrival, to a train to Bela Crkva like we did coming to Smederevo. But no, the trains did not run because the Panchevo bridge across the Danube, that is the bridge from Belgrade to Panchevo and on to Bela Crkva, was blown up a week or so earlier. There was no alternative provided by the railways and here we were, two young boys—with one pretty well an invalid—literally stranded at the useless railway station.

It was everybody-for-himself principle. Luckily, a kind person, seeing our plight, told us that we should go to the Ferry Terminal where we might catch a ferry across Danube to Panchevo. He also explained to us how to find our way to that Terminal.

I must add that it was not safe any more for young children to be about in Belgrade unaccompanied by adults because some had been kidnapped and, literally, made into sausages. Yes, it is true and well documented. A number of gangs involved in these kind of atrocities have been caught and the gruesome details written up in the newspapers for days. Sure, times were tough, but they were tough for everybody. So, how low can a man get before he becomes an animal? I think that was it.

About an hour and a half after we left the railway station, we arrived at the Ferry Terminal to find masses of people, most in

German uniform, waiting for the next ferry. So, when the ferry arrived, everybody tried to get on board and my brother and I just made it on when a unit of German Wermacht soldiers turned up and all civilians were ordered to get off so the new soldiers can get on. I remember we pleaded with the loud-voiced sergeant to let us stay on and I showed him my swollen knee hoping he would be sympathetic, but to no avail as he yelled, 'Get off immediately, or we'll toss you both overboard,' or something like that.

We got off and started to walk—in my case hobble and hop—along the shore to where somebody said we might get a man to take us across in a rowboat, and then: B-O-O-O-M! There was this huge ear-shattering explosion and as we turned around to see what it was, we saw the ferry, now half way across the Danube, alight and sinking fast. By golly, it was a close shave for us that time! We were lucky the loud-voiced sergeant was not sympathetic to my swollen knee and would not let us stay on. I often think of 'what if' he let us stay on board. As we walked farther along the shore we saw some blackened bodies floating by and I wondered if that sergeant was one of them.

Eventually, we saw a man with a rowboat and after some haggling over the price, we got in and he started to row across the river. Although it was late in the day, it being summer it was still light enough to see these dark spheres floating by our boat. We were scared they were mines and we would be blown up like the ferry. But, no, they were just ordinary watermelons(!) that, I guess, came from an overturned boat, and some hardworking farmer would not now be taking them to the markets to sell, or barter for some other goods.

Soon, we arrived at the other side of Danube and jumped on shore, which I remember was very grassy and very tricky for me to walk on without agonising pain in my knee. Actually, I wanted to stop right there and then and not walk anywhere that night.

However, we could see in the distance the main road and some moving cars and trucks on it, and, as dusk was approaching, my brother decided that we must continue and get to the road as quickly as possible. He then asked me to get on his back so he could carry me—and that he did! As I was not light, it must have been quite a feat of strength for him, a mere fourteen year old boy!

After what seemed an age, with many stops, we got to the main road and met up with some other people who were also waiting for a lift to Panchevo. By that time it was dark, but luckily we did not have to wait long before a bus with plenty of room for everyone, stopped and picked us up. Lucky, again! The bus took us to Panchevo and, as it happened, to the railway station—just what we wanted! However, as my knee was by now very sore and throbbing a treat, and the fact that the train to Bela Crkva was not due for a few hours yet, we decided to go to the Panchevo hospital to have it looked at.

The hospital was not too far and we got to it quickly enough. After waiting a while a doctor came, looked at my knee and ordered me to be admitted immediately. That was a big problem! The train to Bela Crkva was leaving in about two hours or so, and God knows when the next one would be—if at all, as things then were definitely in a state of flux.

So, after I was admitted and put to bed—it must have been very late at night—the nurses left the ward for, I guess, a cup of tea or some other refreshment, and I immediately took that opportunity to escape without much of my clothing! Remember, my knee was bad and hurting like blazes, but I somehow managed to get out the back door and find my brother who was waiting at the front of the hospital for something like this to happen, I suppose!

To cut the long story short, we got on the train and arrived in Bela Crkva late in the morning. As we were a few days early to get into the school to enrol etc., we decided to go to the Rumjantsevs' place and ask for help; after all they were Uncle Volodja and Aunt Natasha to us and they also had our memorabilia stored in their attic. Remember?

The Rumjantsevs immediately put me in their spare room and called the lady doctor friend, who came soon enough, had one look at my knee and decided to operate then and there as she had all the necessary articles in her bag. Actually she didn't need much, just some ether as a local anaesthetic, and a scalpel to cut the swelling open and drain the fluid. She didn't stitch the incision and so to this day there it is this 3 x 1 cm scar above my knee for everyone to see and remind me of the impromptu 'operation'.

Actually, I have had a few incisions since, especially lately with my BCC skin cancers, of course always with a local anaesthetic, and I must say the feeling is different. For example, if I think about the Bela Crkva 'operation', to the exclusion of everything else in my mind, I can always feel it exactly as I felt it seventy years ago. Strange that?

So, I stayed at the Rumjantsevs' place for about 7–10 days until the wound healed and the knee was no longer the size of a balloon, but its normal size.

Whilst there I saw a lot of Lena, who brought me nice things to eat like ginger biscuits and apples and stayed with me to talk. As I don't remember what any of the talks were about, I must conclude that they must have been 'small talk', or, also likely, I was not paying any attention.

While I was at the Rumjantsevs, my brother was back in the Cadet School, as the place was open for business earlier than expected. In town there was talk among the White Russian population of fleeing the country and the school was contemplating evacuation to somewhere safer.

Incidentally, I forgot to note that about six months or so earlier, the Germans issued the senior cadets with antiquated rifles to practice rifle skills. It was thought that, should they need to defend the school and other things from the enemy and were issued with modern rifles, they would then only need minimal training to be able to use them competently.

So, with all these rifles about, the scarcity of food, an increased black market activity, an air of concern in town of a precursor-to-panic kind, plus a faint rumbling of gunfire that could be heard 24 hours a day—and was getting louder each day—was for me a replay of the Skopje experience when the Germans were about to enter Yugoslavia, except that this time they were about to flee it!

I left the Rumjantsevs' place, as I said, after about a week or so, and rejoined the Cadet School. Next time I saw the Rumjantsevs was 30 years later in 1973 in Canada. I will always be grateful for their enduring friendship.

By the way, the Rumjantsevs stayed on in Bela Crkva until well after the war. Lena, after finishing high school in Bela Crkva, went to Belgrade University where she met a Ukrainian fellow from Canada, and after marrying him, went to live in Canada. Later, Uncle Volodja and Aunt Natasha joined them when they retired from dentistry and sold out their house in Bela Crkva.

Rumjantsevs in Canada: Welcome dinner for me

At the Rumjantsevs' summer place

When it became clear to the German Command in Yugoslavia that the Red Army's push through Rumania towards Yugoslavia could not be stopped, the order was given for all military to start evacuation. This order to the military seemed to have been tantamount to pressing a general panic button as many inhabitants started to prepare to flee also. Where to? Why? These two questions did not seem to have been seriously considered by many as they were completely overwhelmed by a mob hysteria and followed like sheep. Many regretted their action later when they were exposed in their travels to untold hardship.

For reasons unexplained, but I had my suspicions that they considered us as 'cannon fodder', the Cadet School was deemed by the Germans to be military for the purposes of evacuation. So, one bright morning, with the distant gun fire of the Red Army advancing through Rumania now quite audible, the cadets who were in the school for the start of the new school year—and more than half were not because their parents decided against it, opting to do it their way or stay at home instead—marched to the railway station to board the train to take them to Germany to become part of its military 'human resources', as we later found out. So, my suspicions were correct.

The train that was taking us to Germany was not your passenger train with proper carriages, but a train of 'coal wagons', that is, open wagons with hinged sides that can be tilted to dump any granular material being transported.

If anybody suggests that we did not rate high enough with the German Military for even something like the cattle wagons, I would agree with the suggestion that we did not rate high enough, but I would disagree about the wagons. I think that things were so critical that we were lucky to have any wagons at all—coal, or otherwise!

Anyway, the cadets all got into the last four, or was it five?, wagons and settled in, with some sitting on the floor, some standing and some sitting on the sides dangling their feet in or out, as the case may be. As the few officers and teachers who were single or widowed, including the School Commandant, Major-General Popov, also came along, there seemed to be at least one officer for each wagon. Anyway, we had one in our wagon.

Then after a period of time, the steam locomotive gave a whistle and everybody jumped back into the wagon and we were off into the unknown with a lot of yelling and joking. The train was slow and the hours passed by slowly.

Before we left Bela Crkva we were issued with a food parcel and a bottle of water, so we had 'lunch on the train'.

There was also a can provided in each wagon for when nature called. Of course, there was no enclosure and if you were shy you were in big trouble! Come to think of it there was no lid on the can either! Well, there were no girls there and, anyway, not many of us were shy about these things. Remember the 'N parasha' we had to empty as punishment in our cadet quarters in Bela Crkva?

From Bela Crkva the railway line headed to Vrshats, a town about 80 km or so away and then it turned towards the Hungarian border town of Szeged, or Subotica—meaning "Saturday"—as its name was when that area was part of Yugoslavia. Why 'Saturday' and not 'Friday' for example? I have no idea.

When we got to Szeged, the train stopped just outside the town and it remained so for a long time. We were bored, and while some played cards that some enterprising cadet brought along with him, and some others read books they had, I climbed onto the front side of my wagon and sat on the side with my feet dangling outside to talk to a new cadet in the wagon in front, who was doing a similar thing, namely, sitting on the back side of his wagon with his feet also dangling outside the wagon and facing me.

We talked about this and that and gesticulating when appropriate to do so. Suddenly, without any warning, the train jerked forward to resume its journey north.

As the train jerked forward, I fell into the wagon and the new cadet fell off his wagon and onto the rail with his head on it. As the wheel of our wagon moved on, it crushed his head. Terrible! Terrible! Terrible! If I live 1000 years I will never forget our heavy wagon literally lifting as the boy's head was crushed and seeing the officer in our wagon press his hands against his ears. Although I forgot the officer's name, I can see him as clearly as if he were in front of me now, pressing his hands against his ears to muffle the crushing noise, with an expression on his face of utter disbelief.

I have often thought of what might have happened if the train had jerked backward rather than forward as it did—something that often happens with steam trains starting off. Clearly, it would have been him into the wagon and me onto the rail with my head on it. But … I was lucky again!

This tragedy has had an indelible impact on me. I can still see the boy's mother saying good bye to him on the railway station platform in Bela Crkva and giving him a parcel of goodies to take with him. What would she have thought of her son being killed less than a day later? How did she receive the news? Did she receive the news? And what powerful logic was behind the decision to send him away like this? We will never know the answers to these questions now. Life must go on.

The tragedy that befell our train had the effect of keeping it at the scene of the accident for some 3–4 hours while waiting for the police to arrive, take statements, measure the scene of the accident and make a sketch of it. Eventually we left Szeged, and as we did it was with an air of gloom about what happened so early in our journey. That night we slept in the wagons as the train noisily 'steamed' its way towards Germany.

In our journey towards Germany we must have gone through Budapest, but I don't remember it. I remember Vienna, or rather Wiener Neustadt, that is 'Vienna's Newtown' as it would be in English, which is part of Vienna, but a bit outside of it. I also remember that being the first time we made a comfort stop, and we were quite relieved for this opportunity to get out of the train for a little while.

We then continued on trough Czechoslovakia and I remember we passed through Budweiss as 'Budjovice' was called during the German occupation of Czechoslovakia. I guess, people would immediately recognise Budweiss because of the famous 'Budweisser beer'. 'Budjovice beer' will just fall flat on people's ears. No pun intended!

CHAPTER V

The Luftwaffe Time
(Sept '44 – May '45)

Eventually, we arrived at our destination: a town called Eger in the part of Germany known as Sudetenland. Formerly, this area was part of Czechoslovakia with a dubious reputation of being the first of Hitler's forays into Germany's neighbourhood in his grand plan to rule the world and a litmus test of the world's reaction. History tells us that reaction was: 'Tut, tut, naughty boy! Don't do that again!'—these are my words. The official version, namely, 'Peace in our time,' was announced by Mr Chamberlain, the Prime Minister of Great Britain at that time, after talking to Hitler and getting a promise from him that he will never do that again. How naive can you get, or, if you believe that you'd believe anything!

From the Eger Railway Station we were transported by lorries to the Luftwaffe Complex consisting of a huge airfield with lots of planes and barracks, or rather long huts. On our arrival we were received by two German 'Unteroffiziers', or 'Subofficers' as it would read in English, who were to be in charge of us. Unbelievable that it existed!— this photo documents the event. I am definitely somewhere in the photo near the end of the line, and if not in the first row, then in the second row. I don't think it is important which. The fact is, I was there in person and saw it all, as they say!

Cadets arrival in Eger

The hut beside us in the photo, was our hut and is the kind of hut I referred to above as barracks. Inside the hut was a central corridor and on either side were rooms, holding about twenty or so of us sleeping in bunks three-high.

Incidentally, after we were received here and before we entered our hut we were marched off for 'Entleusung' or delousing. This entailed stripping to our birthday suits and the stripping—that is, uniform, undies, and so on—went that way to be pressure cooked, while we went this way to be disinfected and showered. Afterwards, we were ushered into a store/fitting room and got our Luftwaffe uniforms and things. It was just as well we got them because when we met up with our deloused uniforms, undies, etc., they were pretty well unusable. For example, all our leather items, like the belts that were a proud part of our uniform, as is clear from the photo, were now hard and brittle.

The next stop was getting our mug shots taken, with an ID number hanging from our neck, just like for your police common criminals files. Some days later we actually received our

'Soldbuch', a standard abbreviation for 'Soldaten Buch' or 'Soldier's Book', with our photo in it. Unfortunately, neither I nor my brother kept it because if you were found with one on you by the Allied soldiers, you ran a big risk of being treated impolitely and unsympathetically.

After all the delousing, showering, outfitting and the paperwork was over we had to do a 'march past', as recorded in the next photo.

Cadets march past in Eger

Notice that one of the officers on the podium, on the right, is our own 'GenPop', still in his Russian general's uniform. He had refused to change into the German uniform and was apparently allowed to do so.

The officer on the left on the podium is the German colonel who was the Commandant of the Complex, then next to him is a 'civilian' and behind GenPop is another officer. It is also interesting to see here that we are wearing an armband to say who we are; this was a very practical German method to identify immediately who was who. Remember, that was also what the Schutzkor soldiers of my father had, to signify they were Russians in the German uniform.

After all the initial formalities and processes, we settled into the Eger routine. By now we were approaching the end of October, so it was getting colder and our outdoor morning exercises—bare chested, of course—produced quite a bit of steam around us. For some reason, this steam reminded me of the horses in the stables of my father's cavalry unit in Pozharevats. Funny how that is!

We also did drills, gymnastics, marching and weapon training, all of which we learned by rote as we did not speak much German. After seventy plus years I can still recite *'Das Gewehr acht und vierzig Ka besteht aus sieben Haupteile ... usw'*, that is, that *'The rifle 48K consists of seven main parts ... etc'*. I don't know quite what to make of this fact that I can still remember all that, even though I had not used this information for seventy plus years. What for? Perhaps a neurologist or a neuro-scientist may be able to explain it, or make something of it.

Of course, the best part of our activities in the Complex was to be marched off to the canteen for a meal. Even though the differently coloured soup—the two most frequent colours being off-green and very much off-white—was an everyday 'treat', it never seemed to have anything solid in it. The other 'treat' was the army bread that I already compared with the breads of Nish, especially when it was surfaced with a spread of 'Ersatz Margarine', or 'Substitute Margarine'. All I can say about the stuff is that it was greasy— but so is the stuff used to grease the cart wheels with! The coffee that we always seemed to have had in plentiful supply was actually substitute chicory— invented by some frustrated chemist, I should think! And, of course, we never had any fresh vegetables or fruit.

So, our stomachs were always kind of empty. We used to actually look forward to the air raid sirens going off because that meant we had to march off, or run, as the case may be, to some farmers' fields nearby to sit around waiting for the 'all clear' siren to sound so we could return back to the airfield Complex. The reason we looked forward to these 'outings' was that we often could unearth a 'kohlrabi', as the 'German turnip' was called, left in the ground from the last harvest. They were generally pretty fibrous and stringy things, but who complained? It was a 'fresh' vegetable, and that was good enough.

Interestingly, during that three months of 1944 in Eger, all we ever encountered were air raid alarms and never an actual air raid as such, with bombs and things. That was odd because the airfield was used for fighter planes to take off and 'bother' the B-17s overhead on their way to bomb a local factory, a town, or some place nearby like Karlsbad.

Whenever we were in the fields responding to an air raid alarm, and the skies were clear, which was often so in winter, we got to witness a spectacular sight. The ever so brightly glistening B-17s appeared as specks flying in formation with their vapour trails silhouetted against the blue skies as other the fighter planes buzzed like mad amongst them.

One of our tasks in the winter was to keep the snow away from the runway where the ordinary fighters took off and also from in front of the 'special' plane. Before this propeller-less thing could take off, a large truck came along and inserted a big hose into a hole in the plane's nose and blew in hot air for some 10–15 minutes. Then the aircraft itself made lots of noise, the hose was unhooked, and off it flew trailing the engine noise behind. Unreal!

The thing was, of course, a jet plane. It was the first time we had seen a jet plane, and to see one whizz by noiselessly above and then finally hear the noise and look up to see no plane, was, as I said, unreal. One shortcoming of that jet plane was that it could not stay aloft for much longer than half an hour or so. Why, I don't know. Incidentally, according to my brother it was a 'Jumo' jet. Well, be that as it may, I will not argue with it.

Most of our time, as I already noted above, was spent on drills, gymnastics, marching, weapon training and clearing snow. Other units in the complex—and there was practically a League of Nations there—were doing anti-aircraft training and our older cadets joined in. The younger cadets spent time inside, playing cards, reading, etc. There was one new cadet, who used the cards for fortune telling. Everybody had their fortune told with the most popular being: 'I can see in the cards a parcel of food that you will soon receive from home,' which was pretty much what everybody wanted to hear, so everybody was happy.

My own predicted fortune, however, was strange: 'I can see in the cards that you will soon be in jail'. 'Come on. Get out of it!' I said. 'This is the craziest thing I have ever heard! Anyway, what about my food parcel? Don't I get one?' So, I didn't bother about his stupid fortune telling again. Silly boy. Me go to jail. Tell me another one!

A couple of times during our stay in the Eger Complex, we were allowed to go to town as part of our recreation. It was more an education than recreation. We certainly were not of an age 'to paint the town red', nor did we have the money to do it. The best we could do is 'look-see', sit in the restaurant and drink 'coffee'—read 'chicory'—only, as for any side helping you needed a food coupon and we did not have them. As we discovered, the only thing you could buy in a shop that did not require coupons was mustard— and it was cheap! We bought quite a bit of it and used it on the army bread as a spread. It was German mustard and nothing like your English mustard that takes your breath away and kills cold and flu germs instantly dead. Instead, in both taste and colour it was almost like the French mustard.

One strange contraption that we came across in the town was a wall dispenser of something I remember called 'Olagum'. We at first thought they were cough lollies of some sort, but later found out that they were condoms. These wall dispensers were to be found in strategic locations and not, as with us in Australia, in public toilets only. Remember, the year was 1944, when sex education was non-existent and if you wanted to buy a condom you went to the chemist and whispered it. I consider this thing we saw in Eger progressive and educational and well ahead of other countries at the time.

With all this shortage of proper food, minerals and vitamins, many people suffered effects of these deficiencies of one kind or other. Mine was boils. I had them everywhere on my body and they lasted for weeks. In the complex's hospital they gave me a cream to put on them—a black goo that not only smelled like tar, but most probably was tar! So, I walked around smelling like a council worker who has been asphalting holes in the road all day. Boils in Russian are 'chiriki' and when I was asked what I had, I stammered out 'chi-chi-chiriki'. Of course, I was teased with it for months. Not nice. As I walked by, my friends would say to each other, 'Look, there goes chi-chi'. Some friends!

Soon it was December and with it came plenty of snow. One punishment for misdemeanour dished out to us was 'push-ups-on-the-run'. This entailed us running a few metres and on the command 'Hin', getting down on the ground, or snow as the case may be, and doing a few push-ups and then on the command 'Auf', getting up, running a few metres, and repeating all that again and again, until the officer had enough. In fact, he often did not bother to issue the command 'up-down', but just moved his thumb back and forth 90° and you were supposed to keep track of it. Look out if you made a mistake! Army is a tough world, especially for a twelve and a half year old boy.

Well, Christmas was soon just a week away. The cadets agreed we needed to do something festive to spruce up our quarters and a Christmas tree was high on the list. It was something not so hard to come by as most of the forests around were pine tree forests. So, we got a tree and made up some home-made decorations that looked very nice ... but what about the candles? Christmas tree lights, as we have now, did not exist then and candles were the traditional lights on Christmas trees—needless to say many a Christmas tree has gone up in flames before the actual end of the Christmas festivities!

So, what shall we do? 'Ah ...,' somebody said, 'the airfield is full of parked "Savoia Marchetti" planes that were going nowhere; surely we can get some control panel bulbs from them and a car/truck battery and make us some Christmas tree candles'. What a brilliant idea!

'Savoia Marchetti' planes were the three engine Italian transport planes and there were, literally, hundreds of them, neatly parked on the edge of the airfield. They were parked there when we arrived in Eger and they never flew. That was because of the fuel shortage, which I commented upon in connection with the bombing of the Ploeshti oil fields in Rumania and the Smederevo refinery when my brother and I were visiting our father in his guardhouse there.

Next—and I really do not remember why!—Michael Chernyi, Michael Gontcharov and I were selected to go and unscrew us some control panel bulbs from the Savoia Marchettis. So, we got ourselves a pen knife each and waited for the evening so it would be dark and we would not be spotted. The two Michaels were older than me. Michael Gontcharov was fourteen and a bit and Michael Chernyi would have been not far from fourteen.

When it got dark, we left our hut with all the cadets giving advice, loudly and all at once, of what to do and how and what to look out for. Really? If you know so much, you go! Anyway, we went and got to a plane we homed in on, without any problems. There were no guards to be seen, so we tried to get into the plane, but it was not easy. The doors were locked and we could not open them. So, we went to the next plane and tried there. Same! Then one of the Michaels suggested a direct attack, namely, through the pilot's window. I ought to note that we did not have torches, but could still see things well enough because it was clear skies and enough moonlight. But the same moonlight also helped the guards see the planes well from where they were some distance away. We were too occupied trying to loosen the cockpit window with our pen knives to see that one of the guards was coming to investigate. When we saw him, we jumped down and started to run.

As I already noted in the Prologue, the two Michaels were caught running away from the plane while I must have ran faster and escaped back to the hut and got into my bunk trembling a treat. About an hour later the unit was woken up and everybody lined up in the corridor. Two German officers asked who was the third boy involved and ordered that he step to the front. After a long minute of silence nobody stepped out, so they got really angry and the senior officer yelled again and pulled his revolver out of its holster —he was definitely not going to be messed about by a bunch of boys at 11 o'clock at night two days before Christmas! Then I stepped out, or was actually pushed out, as I remember it. The rest is back in the Prologue.

The last thing I said in the Prologue was that the duty guard officer said that we were to be shot. We cried, of course. As we were being interrogated, all the questions and our answers were translated by an ad-hoc translator from Ukraine; actually from Galitsia, the ex-Polish part, so his Russian was not very good, and

I suspect his German also, because the Germans decided to lock us up and continue the interrogation the next day with the proper translator. Besides, it was late and everybody wanted a rest. So, we were marched down the stairs to the back of the ground floor where the cells were and locked up in the cell— all three of us in the one cell. The accuracy of the fortune teller haunts me still.

The guards there were pretty good to us and pretty lax, but that was I think because they could see that we were just kids and maybe some of them had kids like us back at home. As it turned out we were not called the next day for more interrogation and, in fact, not only the next day, but never. I guess, the next day being Christmas Eve people were thinking more about Christmas than those three naughty kids. Also, I suspect that the duty guard officer who interrogated us and was going to have us shot, was no longer there, as a week or so later the lock-up was visited by a new officer. This officer must also have been from the same strict school as the previous guy, because after his visit, we were each put in a separate cell and when we wanted to go to the toilet the guard came, pulled out the 'Mauser' from his holster, opened the door and escorted us one at a time up to the toilet.

When I now think of me, a small twelve year old boy, being escorted by this big guy with this big revolver almost pressed against my back, I can't stop laughing because, if you think about it, the scene does look incongruous and ridiculous—like a scene from a Charlie Chaplin silent movie.

What did we do there in the jail all day long? And what about the food?

The last bit first: if my brother did not organise some food for us, by collecting little from each cadet back in the hut, and got it to us each day on a long pole through the tiny cell window, we would have seriously starved, as the lock-up food appeared only irregularly and when it did it was not very wholesome.

What did we do? Well, when we were together in the same cell we talked and horsed around, which was good as it was a kind of exercise. We were not let out for exercise. Luckily it was warm enough in the cells. As regards exercise, I am sure there must have been a Geneva Convention about exercise for prisoners like us, but it must have been only a piece of paper with no teeth, or the Eger Luftwaffe people have not heard of it, or something like that. Of course, something that we did every day was squash lice in our undies and on our heads, but that's hardly the exercise I was referring to!

Of course, when we got split up and put into single cells we couldn't get at the lice on our heads, but only in the undies. Needless to say, the undies had quite an odour and could just about stand by themselves—they were of that kind of consistency. Well, we did not have a shower or a bath that winter, so no wonder we were like that. However, there was still a chance yet of a shower or a bath that winter—after all, we were still only half way through the winter!

The other activity that I remember we did while in jail was dig trenches somewhere on the other side of town next to a large building. I don't know what for or for whom, but 'Befehl ist Befehl', or 'Orders are Orders'. Have you ever tried digging frozen ground? Not the easiest thing at the best of time. But when you are a twelve year old boy, malnourished and full of lice and boils—it's tough!

We were in this jail with lack of food, exercise, etc., completely ignored by the guards, it seemed till about the mid-January 1945.

What happened then was we were released and sent back to our hut to join the other cadets. This was most odd and unexpected. After all, we were supposed to have been on what is commonly known in most prisons as 'the death row'. There is one version of why we were released that I was told. It goes something like this.

General Vlasov was visiting his airforce pilots in Eger. He was a big shot and was not to be upset or angered in any way. One thing that might have upset or angered him was the three Russian cadet soldiers, namely us, being kept in the cells. So, the Germans released us with the idea of locking us back up again after General Vlasov had left. Next, a bit about who the good general was and why.

In the beginning of the war with USSR, many citizens in USSR and the Red Army personnel saw the Germans as liberators from Stalin's oppression and were not fighting the Germans seriously and, in fact, were surrendering in droves. Had the Germans been smarter and not upset and angered the civilian population in USSR and the POWs, but understood the Russian psychology a bit better, the world now may have been quite a different place from what it is. For a starter, German would have been the international language, instead of English, and I don't know about the 'euro' and the 'yen'. Would they still be with us? Probably.

Of the Red Army that the Germans confronted, one big chunk was under the command of General Vlasov. He surrendered his army to them with the idea of then turning back and fighting the bad guys in the Red Army, whom everybody hated, and not the ordinary soldiers who would have gone over to become the 'Vlasovtsi' , or the 'Vlasov's boys', at the drop of a hat. Well, the Germans apparently couldn't have learnt well from my father's army, the 'Schutzkor', and seemed to have made the same mistake by getting the Vlasov's boys to fight armies other than the hated Red Army commissars. So, Vlasov's army became simply a bigger version of the 'Schutzkor', with some tank units and fighter squadrons—the latter being stationed in Eger.

To reiterate, the 'Schutzkor' consisted of the genuine 'White Army' personnel like my father, who were royalists, supporting Tzar Nicholas II and fighting the Bolsheviks of the 'Red Army'.

The 'Red Army' that the Germans confronted in the beginning of the war with USSR was in reality not that, but what I would describe as the 'Pink Army'. It consisted of men of the 'Red Army' who had had enough of Stalin and his Bolshies, and if given the opportunity would have joined the 'White Army', and turned back on the 10% or so of the remaining and hated, hard core communists.

The credence to what I am describing above may be seen right now in the democratic Russia. The flag, white-blue-red, is royalist, the Russian Orthodox religion is back and the churches are full, the nephew of Tzar Nicholas II has been invited to Russia with a view to restarting the monarchy, etc. In short, more than 90% of the Russians have never in their hearts accepted communism. They were just hibernating for sixty years. If the Germans were cleverer it could have been twenty five years—that's all!

So, there you are—believe it or not, as they say. Believe what? Believe all of the above plus that the Germans released us kids from the jail because of General Vlasov and would have locked us back again after he had left. Well, they were just not fast enough for that, because on the next day, the whole Cadet unit got moved to Gmünd, a town some 200 km away, and, of course, we went along. So, even if we were to have been locked up again, it was not possible because we were no longer there in Eger, but in Gmünd. How convenient! Why the unit was moved to Gmünd, I don't know—just orders, I guess.

¶

In Gmünd we were barracked in a large building that had previously been a school, just like our old School building in Bela Crkva that was taken over by the German army for their barracks. It was cold. Well, it was winter, after all.

A few days later, the three of us, that is, the two Michaels and I, were called up to the commanding officer. He told us that he had received orders from Eger that we were not to be let loose, but kept under surveillance, because our case was still one of attempted sabotage and what to do with us was still to be determined.

Now, let's get this in the correct perspective. Here we are at the end of January 1945. Things are going badly for the German Army just about everywhere. The Allied armies are fast approaching our location. They are bombing factories and towns, left right and centre and have the complete freedom of the skies. And here, the Germans are still hounding three kids for a minor misdemeanour. Have they got their priorities all wrong, or what? As will be apparent later when I recount an 'eleventh-hour case', military rules and discipline are enshrined in stone and there cannot be any exceptions—no matter how stupid or unrealistic the following of the rules and discipline can sometimes actually be.

So, we had left Eger in a hurry and were now in Gmünd and I didn't know why, nor for that matter did anyone else know why. If I were asked what would be the most memorable experience I had in Eger, what would I say? I would say that all my experiences in Eger were most memorable. People might say, 'But, you can't have that! In the English language, if you say 'most memorable' there's got to be one only and no more.' OK, so I will rephrase things a bit and give you my number one most terrifying experience, and it is one that I have not described so far, but it is memorable all right!

You may remember in connection with air raids my saying that all of the time in the last quarter of 1944 in Eger, all we ever encountered were air raid alarms and never an actual air raid as such, with bombs and things. I also thought that was odd because the airfield was used for fighter planes to take off and 'bother' the B-17s overhead. Well, I suppose you've already guessed it: they did bomb the airfield ... when we three kids were locked up in the cells and everyone else ran away to the air raid shelter and left us stranded there. Now, that was a very, very frightening experience! I was in the cell alone. There was a small window, the size of a couple of house bricks, high up in the wall. You could not see anything, but, by golly, you could hear the bombs exploding all around and you were just waiting for one to hit the lock-up—and you. You want to escape instantly, now and immediately, but you can't. You are like a frightened animal in a cage, running from one side to the other, pulling at the door, but it won't budge. Luckily, no bomb hit us, but it is the sort of experience you read about that turns men grey overnight. Sure, I was just a kid, I did not go grey, but I also can't say it had no effect on me, because it did. But, as I noted before, life must go on.

Back in Gmünd we seemed to have done nothing else, but continuously responding to air raid alarms and marching, or running, as the case may be, to a forest that was not too far away. I remember there was a small lake, or a big pond, if you like, at the edge of the forest, the size of my beloved lake in Bela Crkva, and that brought back memories of fishing, etc. There was ice on the edge of the lake, but one day some of our cadets decided to strip off and horse around in it. I didn't. Luckily, there were no consequences either way— nobody got punished and nobody caught a cold.

One day, we were sheltering in the forest again when we heard some loud aeroplane noise and there were some twin fuselage fighter planes (American 'Lightnings'), flying very low strafing a train couple of kilometres away. As I looked up—from behind a tree, of course!— I momentarily could see the pilot in it. That was a new experience and something to remember. Incidentally, the train they were strafing must have carried some ammunition, as soon afterwards there were a few loud explosions coming from the direction of where the railway line went by.

So, days and weeks went by and things were really hotting up. By now, I was becoming good at recognising the tell-tale signs of the coming military and subsequent occupation of the town/ country. For a starter, the food was scarce, people in the streets were walking just that bit faster, the worried look on their faces was permanent, there were more or less continuous blackouts, etc. And I was right. One day, we were told that the cadet unit will be marching to München, which was our next destination as ordered by the HQ. What HQ? What will we do in München? Who else will be there? 'That's too many questions you silly boy.' one may say. And that's true. If you want an answer you can get one. That's easy. It is: 'Befehl ist Befehl', or 'Orders are Orders'.

And that's how it was. Nobody ever explained who this magic order-giving person was. Was he a competent order-giver, or just a mediocre one? What qualification did he have to give orders? What experience did he have? What was his success rate? And this last bit was important for the survival of our cadet unit. If his success rate was not good, we would be goners.

For some reason or other, together with about three other cadets, I was declared unfit to march the five hundred kilometres from Gmünd to München. Please note it was Gmünd not Gmünden, which is another town altogether! So, the fit lot will march and the weaklings, or, unfit lot, which I prefer to use, will go by train. The latter is easy to say. Anybody can say 'Go by train'. No problem to say it, but a colossal problem to actually do it in March 1945 in Gmünd, with the Allied forces coming rapidly towards the place, and their planes strafing trains and blowing up railway lines and bridges. But orders are orders—and that's that! You have to go by train to München. Full Stop. Capital letter!

So, the next day, as my brother and the other cadets started on their march to München, I and three other 'unfit' cadets, went to the railway station to get on a train that was heading as closely, or as roughly, in the München direction, as possible. Ha … but we were not the only ones with that idea. There must have been a thousand others! Eventually, I and at least one other cadet just made it on to the roof of one train, and off we went! Nothing to hang on to on the roof. Good thing it was not raining, not that getting wet would have been the worst thing: it was falling off a slippery roof that would have been disastrous. As I remember it, the train was slow, because, I suppose, the driver was on the lookout for damaged rails and wanted to be sure he could stop the train in time. Full marks! So, we chugged along at a running speed.

Then, and I can't remember whether it was the same day or the next day, the train stopped because some trigger happy Allied fighter pilots wanted to have some strafing practice. Well, you wouldn't have seen a train emptying anywhere any faster than our train did. Everybody just took off into the fields on either side of the railway track. I did, too, but for some reason I could not run as fast as I used to. Maybe the decision that I was unfit to march to München was right, after all. As it turned out, it was a blessing in disguise, because the planes just made two passes without doing much damage, I guess they saw it was mainly civilians, and flew off to practice strafing some place else.

The train drivers, having, I am sure, already had experience of being strafed before, did not run far either and as soon as the planes flew off they got back into the train and started off without waiting for everybody to come back. Well, there were people running after it like mad and yelling to the driver to stop, but he didn't. Maybe that was the rule, I don't know—but it was certainly cruel to those who didn't make it back. One advantage for me and another cadet, Gabriel Sodbinow, about a year older than me, was that we got inside the carriage and actually got a seat each. We didn't see the other two cadets since. They must have been left behind in the fields.

Which towns and regions we were passing in the next week, or even two, is somewhat hazy in my mind. We did not speak German. We did not have any maps with us. We did not know the local geography. The best we were hoping for is that the trains we were on from time to time were going in more or less the direction of München. After all, as I said before, there was about five hundred kilometres from Gmünd to München. Additionally, Gmünd is on the Czechoslovakia-Germany border and München is in Bavaria and there is Austria in between.

The other thing Gabriel and I were aiming to do was stick together so we wouldn't be separated. That was not easy. Remember, each had to go to the toilet some time and there were people packed tightly everywhere, so there was pushing and shoving on the way. Good thing we had only the small rucksacks on our backs. Well, it was good for this purpose, but not good for other purposes. There was no food in the rucksacks and not much clothing either.

Quite frankly, I was in a confused state for pretty well this entire journey. I was tired and hungry. The train kept stopping two or three times a day because of damaged lines or strafing, in which case people left the train to hide nearby. I never went too far for fear of being left behind. Also, we had to change trains frequently, and it was during one of these changes my greatest fear was realised: Gabriel and I got separated. I clearly remember what happened. It was night time. We arrived at a station of a town the name of which I don't know, but which I called then—and still call—'The town-at-an-intersection'. Why this name, God knows.

I was dog tired. Inside the waiting room it was hot and packed with people. Then a train arrived and Gabriel and I got on it somehow. As the train pulled out of the station and started gathering speed, the thought flashed through my mind that it was going in the opposite direction to München, so I jumped off it and nearly hit the signal post in the process. But all that I got out of it was bruises. Lucky again!

I walked back to the station and immediately fell asleep. When I woke up in the morning there were still a lot of people there amongst whom I saw a man and a woman in Russian style uniforms inquiring about something at the ticket window. I immediately approached them and asked where they were going, hoping it was to München. But no, they were a battalion of Cossacks going to Italy and had a train all to themselves waiting on the siding just a couple of hundred metres from the station. They took me with them and gave me some food to eat and then asked, 'Why don't you come with us? We are going to Italy because we will be safe there. The war is just about over, anyway'. I was tempted. I can tell you, with all that food and comfort. But, orders are orders! I was ordered to go to München and that's what I must do—even if it kills me!

I was certainly an outstanding example of discipline to behold and a pride and joy to any military. But, remember, I had two years in the Cadet School, so I was already ahead with the discipline bit. One may argue that discipline is nothing but blind obedience or brain-washing, or both. But in the military it must be so. The military cannot operate any other way. If you want to use your brain and analyse orders, then my advice would be, 'Become a commanding general as soon as possible,' otherwise, keep quiet and follow orders!

So, I again walked back to the station. With all this walking back to the same railway station anyone would think that I would know the name of it in my sleep. But no, I don't. God knows, I have tried. Many years later I have looked at detailed maps trying to recreate the journey, but I always failed. The names are just blanks in my memory. I waited many hours back at the station— in fact, until it was evening and dark again, but no train came.

During this waiting, I remember, a man came into the station and told people that a train full of Cossacks was blown up as it was crossing over a bridge some 30 km away. I did not understand when he gave details of what actually happened to the train, but I understood the first bit about it being blown up. If true—and I have no reason to doubt it—then I was lucky yet again!

Later on in the night, a train heading in the direction to München stopped at the station. I went out to look, but it was a goods train. 'Well,' I said to myself, 'and what's wrong with that? It is going in the right direction. Isn't it? I have been at this place one day and what did I achieve? Nothing'. So, I gingerly opened the door of one wagon, enough for me to slide in. There was straw on the floor in the wagon and that was 'just what the doctor ordered'. The train soon started off and I fell into deep sleep on the straw. I woke up when I heard some voices and other commotion outside. It was daylight again and I could see through the crack in the side; there were some soldiers carrying flat wooden boxes out of the nearby wagons and putting them in some waiting army trucks.

I was curious at all this activity outside. Then it occurred to me to look under the straw that I was sleeping on. So, I removed some of the straw from under me and looked and saw the same boxes there, too. They were gun shells! So, I slept all night on these gun shells that could have gone off at any time! I immediately crawled out the other side and walked to what I saw was a railway station some distance away. Later, it dawned on me what happened and because it was night time, the trigger happy strafing pilots were at home sleeping and getting ready for the daylight to practice their skills on some train or other. Luck was still on my side, it seemed.

At the station I had some 'coffee' and some bread and salami that the thoughtful Cossacks gave me to put in my rucksack 'for a rainy day'. Gee, I hope they weren't all blown up with the train. They were such nice people.

By this time I have lost count of how many days I was travelling—it felt like ages! I don't remember how long I waited at this station, nor, again, its name. Then a train that seemed to be heading in the right direction, pulled up and I jumped on. The next morning—and I remember this well—we were in Salzburg. So, I was in Austria and München now was not that far. Hopefully, I would be in München the next day, or the day after. I wondered if the marching cadets and my brother would be there already. But, wait! Nobody told me where in München I should report. München is a big place. Oh, well, something will turn up.

As the train was pulling into Salzburg station there was an air raid alarm and people were running in all directions. An additional spur to the alarm for the people to run was the fact that the station had already been bombed, as there were damaged buildings and railway tracks everywhere. So, I got out of the train with the mob and followed them to an air raid shelter—a cave/tunnel that had been excavated in a nearby hill and there we waited for the all clear siren to tell us it's all over until the next time. And in the next few weeks there were lots of 'next times'! It was now middle-ish April and things were really hotting up in earnest.

In the air raid shelter I came across none other than Gabriel. What a coincidence! He, like me was following the orders to get to München and, also like me, hoped to get there in the next day, or two. However, it was clear that there was no way we could do that, because the railway line and the main rail bridge across the river Salzach were destroyed. The trains mostly accumulated in Salzburg, but a few, it seems went back. I don't know why. But I wouldn't be surprised if they, too, were following orders.

Also in the air raid shelter there was a unit of the Vlasov's army, but I am not sure whether Gabriel was already with them, or if he was alone until I met him and then we both joined with the unit. Anyway, we became their mascots, or something like that.

The unit commander was a young lieutenant, this side of 30, a nice man with a terrific smile who cared about his soldiers and everybody liked him and, I am sure, would have given their life for him. There were also a few female soldiers in the unit.

The unit seemed to be kind of on its own. One would have thought that a military unit in German uniform and approved by the Highest Command as being for all practical purposes, German, would be bivouacked in a proper military area, But no, they commandeered—if this is the right word—a two storey house in town that was damaged a bit in a bombing raid and empty. Also, they did not seem to have any duties, like guarding, preparing for a battle against the coming Allied army, doing drills, etc. However, they seemed to have enough food for themselves and for the two of us, that is, Gabriel and me. So we were happy enough. Some days we would go with a few of the men for reconnoitring of the town and on other days we would stay with them in the house and watch them play 'Durachok' or 'Fool'—a traditional Russian card game that all Russians, and those aspiring to become Russians, know well.

Gabriel and I did not always go everywhere together; often I would do one thing and Gabriel, another. One occasion that I remember extremely well was when I went with a female soldier to town. I guess, she had this mothering instinct and felt sorry for me, a pathetic looking undernourished kid with a stammer, and asked me along because she wanted to buy something nice for me.

Somewhere along the way we met a Vlasov's army guy on a German military pushbike. The girl soldier seemed to know him, so they talked a bit and then we all went to what seemed to be his flat. Then the man said that he would make 'zakuska'—a typical Russian hoers d'oeuvre—so that they could have it with vodka. Sorry, that's the wrong way round! Vodka comes before zakuska. If you don't have vodka there is no need for zakuska, unless, of course, you go against tradition!

Anyway, they also needed bread, but did not have any. The guy said, 'Why don't we send the kid to get it, while we prepare the zakuska? I will give him the coupons and money'. Upon hearing this I jumped up and said, 'Great, I'll go on the bike!' The guy did not like that idea one bit. I could tell by the zany look on his face. However, the girl said, 'Oh, let him, he is all right. He can ride the bike'. In the end the girl won and I went off on the bike, happy as Larry. After what happened to be described soon, how I wish the guy won and I went on foot. But, in retrospect, thinking about it as an adult, I guess the guy wanted me out of the way so he can smooch up to the girl, so he let me use the bike against his better judgement. I remember his parting words: 'Look after the bike. Don't let it get stolen'.

I rode the bike to where they said the bakery was. I parked the bike outside, so I could keep an eye on it. Unfortunately I could not lock it because it did not have a lock on it. So, my turn in the queue came to be served and I asked for one small bread loaf. As the lady was wrapping it for me, I looked outside only to see a one-legged man hopping on my bike with his crutches up in the air, about to take off. I ran out of the shop fast as lightning and started chasing him and yelling, 'Thief, Thief, Thief', but he was too fast and got away. What a disaster! What an absolute disaster! How could I go back to the guy's flat without his bike? He would murder me, for sure. And at that moment I really would have welcomed it.

So, for the next many hours, I don't know how many, I combed the town from one end to the other, but to no avail. I gave up exhausted, and sat down on the pavement and cried and cried. In the end I went back to the guy's flat to face the music. As I entered the flat I had this vision of him strangling me immediately, for sure. However, although he was mad with me, surprisingly, not aggressively so. When I grew up and became an adult, I got to understand that smooching can have such an effect. Lucky again!

Somewhere in between all these things that were happening to me I must have had my thirteenth birthday. I don't remember celebrating it. It was just another day and a struggle to survive.

¶

The war ended in Salzburg on 12 May 1945. Before then, two things happened that are unforgettable.

First, one morning, on about the 6–7 May, with Gabriel and me still part of the Vlasov unit, a German 'Feldpolizei', or military police unit, arrived and ordered us all out of the house and lined up on the street. As they stood there, stern, expressionless faces, with their submachine guns ready, their tell-tale insignia, a boomerang-like, curved, silvery metal plate, with the words 'Feldpolizei' embossed on it, hung on their chests from a chain round their necks. glistening in the sun. A really frightening scene. Then the commander unrolled a piece of paper and loudly read that the unit had been observed looting some shops for food and that looting was absolutely forbidden and punishable by death. Then upon a lightning command by the officer who read the piece of paper, about half a dozen military police marched up to the Russian unit commander—the young lieutenant—and escorted him to the back of the house. The shots rang in our ears as they executed him. I will never forget the way his soldiers immediately tensed and were almost ready to jump on the German military police then and there even if it cost them their life. I am glad they kept their cool and didn't jump at the military police, because they would have indiscriminately gunned us all down with their submachine guns. That was the kind of charged atmosphere prevailing there at the time.

When I look back at this episode I think what a shame. He was such a nice young man. And if he could have hung on for only another week or so, when the Allied army came to Salzburg, he would still be alive. It was that close. And it was sad. As his soldiers said, he fought with them on many fronts and survived, only to be shot by the military police in this way for what his soldiers thought was an insignificant misdemeanour.

This, then, is the eleventh-hour case I referred to when I was talking about Gmünd and the rules and the discipline the Germans applied to us three kids. It may be worth re-reading.

The second unforgettable thing—and much happier than the first—was as follows. For the next few days or so, after the Vlasov soldiers buried the body of the young lieutenant in the back yard, nobody wanted to stay around that house more than necessary. I wandered around the town, looking at any shop windows that might have still been undamaged and have goods in them on display. Interestingly, during my first week in Salzburg there were a few bombing raids, but after that—none. So it was quite safe to wander along the streets far from air raid shelters.

There were a lot of people in town and crowds of soldiers in one or the other of the many German army uniforms: the steel grey of the Wermacht, the light brown of the army engineers, and so on. In fact, the only uniform missing was the German Navy and that's understandable because Salzburg is a thousand plus kilometres from the nearest sea. If it wasn't for the war the whole thing would appear not only colourful, but also festive. Now and then, as I got tired of walking and needed a rest, I popped into a restaurant or a café for a cup of 'coffee'. I continue to put the word coffee in inverted comas, because it would be a misnomer to label coffee the liquid that was served by that name. As I noted before, the stuff was a ghastly chicory tasting liquid; about the only good thing about it was that it was served hot.

On one of these cup of 'coffee' excursions, I entered a café, and, as per usual it was crowded enough. I found an empty seat and placed my order. As the waiter brought my drink, he asked me to pay for it. That's OK. That's usual. However, as I put my hand into my pocket to get the money out, there was none—the pocket was empty. Somehow, the money must have fallen out during my walk before I got to the café. Well, the waiter became aggressive, raising his voice and generally making himself objectionable. He created quite a scene. I really did not intend to get a free beverage. It was an honest error.

As this kerfuffle was going on, people at the other tables started looking up to see what the problem was, and I looked back at them hoping somebody would help me. At one table I saw some German officers sitting, drinking 'coffee' and 'Schnapps'— the German whisky equivalent—laughing and generally being merry. As I looked a bit more carefully at them, I could see one German 'Hauptman', or a captain, looking at me intensely and then ... jumped up and almost ran towards me. It was my father! I was speechless! The emotion overflowing. We embraced. He paid the waiter. Then we went to his table, he introduced me to his friends and then excused himself and we both left to go to his place. It was a bedroom-sitter on a third floor in some oldish looking building.

What a surprise meeting my father! Absolutely and utterly unexpected! A billion to one chance, if not lots more! After all, we last saw each other in Smederevo where he was an ordinary private, guarding the refinery on the shores of Danube. But this was nine months later in Salzburg, a long way from Smederevo and in another country altogether. He was now a captain and not a private—and that's a big jump in such a short time in anybody's language!

The first thing my father asked was, 'Where is Serge?' I told him what had happened to my brother, how we separated and how he was marching to München, and how I had travelled by trains and so on. Then he told me that after Smederevo he put his name down for an officers' course in some part of Germany. He had recently graduated and was promoted to captain and was on his way, with the other officers, to his new posting and, like me, he got stuck in Salzburg.

I remember well my father opening his suitcase and pulling out a tin of beef and a bottle of schnapps to celebrate the reunion. I did not drink the schnapps, of course, but I had the beef, which must have been off, because I had the runs for the next couple of days.

When now, as a metallurgist, I think about the tin from that 'tin of beef', as I remember it, its colour was more like that of lead than of tin. So, no wonder I had the runs. Lucky it was not worse, that is, a fully-fledged lead poisoning!

As the remaining few days went by we stayed pretty much indoors. Then, it was all over! The Allied tanks, crewed by American Negro units, trundled through the Salzburg streets, without much resistance. I particularly noted the Negroes because that was most unusual for me. Previously, the only Negroes I had seen were in a circus in Skopje.

As the Allied units entered Salzburg, my father opened his suitcase again, took out a civilian suit he had in it, put it on and ceremoniously put his German officer's uniform including the revolver, in a bag and took the bag out and disposed of it somewhere in the back yard.

Then just as ceremoniously, he took out his 'Soldbuch'—the army ID—book and other incriminating documents and cut them all up in little pieces and flushed them down the toilet. I really remember that as if it had happened yesterday. I guess, because it was something very unusual which I have never seen my father do before.

So, that was the end of the war for me and a start of a new chapter in my life.

I survived!

CHAPTER VI
The Austrian Years (1945 — 1949)

And so, the war had ended for me and my father in Salzburg. But where was my brother? Was he still alive? We did not know and at that time there was no way of finding out. If you think about it, my meeting my father was nothing short of a miracle. There were many people who did not know where their loved ones were and, in fact, for many it took years to find them, or their graves as the case may be—and with some they never did. After all, people had moved from one country to another without anyone knowing exactly in which country the war would end for them. I didn't know. My father didn't' know. It was just a matter of chance.

And don't forget, there were four Allied armies and therefore four zones in the 'ex-Greater Germany', if I can call it that. My father and I were lucky to be in the American Zone, but there were also British, Soviet (generally called Russian) and French zones. Also, there was no such thing then as internet, satellite communication, and such like. And even if there was, it would not have been very effective because much of the infrastructure was destroyed. Farms, buildings, power stations, electricity transmission lines, water reticulation, schools, and so on.

When the war ended, all of central Europe was essentially in ruins. The most urgent task was to feed the indigenous population in each country and in some others, especially Germany and Austria, also the millions of refugees to whom, like to me, these countries were their final destination—by order, like with me, or by 'choice' as with those following the panicky mob.

Finding the loved ones was not the top priority for the Occupying Army Administration, but it was to the people trying to find their loved ones, of course. And here the Red Cross and the wall posters that sprung up everywhere did much to bring the many separated ones together. There were hundreds of posters comprising one page 'Have you seen this person' pleas with the person's photo and particulars, placed in locations like railway stations, public places and the like. My father and I had one put up for my brother and then waited for some news. In many cases it was hopeless, but we were optimistic. And that you must always be!

Our first few weeks of 'liberation' were spent scrounging for food. We 'holed up' in a bombed-out, half-ruined house, which was our base for forays into the neighbourhood to look for food and cigarette butts. Cigarettes were the 'hard currency' and cigarette butts were the next best thing. You could exchange them for food very easily and readily and at any time. Unfortunately, my father was a smoker, so most of the time my hard earned 'hard currency' literally went up in smoke! Incidentally, one had to be alert all the time: one, to get to the cigarette butt first and, two, when buying them.

With the latter, it was not even sufficient to open the top of the packet to check that it did in fact contain cigarettes, and not straw dust. You actually had to pull each cigarette out and examine it. Many a time you would open the top of the packet of cigarettes and, yes, it's OK, that's them, only to find later that what you were seeing were short cut up lengths backed by straw dust.

The 'modus operandi' for obtaining cigarette butts was by following an American soldier who was smoking a cigarette and waiting for him to flick it off. And as you were one of maybe as many as ten kids with sometimes one or two adults, you had to be ready to pounce on it first. Here, skill, speed and anticipatory analysis of the smoker's movement plus some knowledge of basic physics, won the day. After some experience you ranked the smokers according to a 'yes — no — maybe' category, meaning was he a candidate worth following, or one not to waste your time on, or you were uncertain. Generally, Negro soldiers were the best and their cigarette butts were also the longest, and officers were the worst. Smokers who threw their cigarette butt on the ground and then twisted it into the ground with their boot were not considered by us to be human.

As to getting the food, there were a number of ways we did it, namely:

1) By standing at the wire fence of a military mess, near the garbage bins, with a tin in your hand stuck through the fence and waiting for the soldiers to scrape their left-overs into your tin, rather than into somebody else's tin, or as some did, into the garbage bin, before they proceeded to the washing-up station. Success here required skill, cunning and experience, and if you had an exceptionally long arm then that was a definite advantage, because you were competing with hundreds of men, women and children, all pushing, jostling and yelling at the same time, 'Please, Please, Please'. As a rule your tin would receive all of the soldier's left-overs which had been in the different compartments in his army plate: soup, bits of the main course, sweets and often his cigarette butt, as well. Even so, it always tasted ever so delicious! When you are perpetually hungry, it is like that.

2) By rummaging through garbage bins around town in places like the backs of restaurants, cafes, hotels and any other building that looked like there were people in it who might throw something edible out.

3) By going to the city dump and rummaging through the garbage there for something edible.

4) By standing near an American GI base or a PX store—the name of military stores where the soldiers could buy all sorts of goodies like cigarettes, chocolate, chewing gum, and such like—and begging for anything at all. You soon learnt how to make your face look so pathetic that no GI could pass you by without giving you something. But, here again you had to compete against a hundred or so other kids and adults!

5) By going to the local farms to look in the ground for left-over potatoes and other root vegetables.

6) By standing under a tree and waiting for a fruit to 'fall down', or its equivalent on the road, namely waiting there for something to 'fall from the back of a truck'.

Needless to say, the last method was the most dangerous one and one that was absolutely the last resort method when you were very, very hungry, and the previous five methods did not produce anything of substance for some days.

Because I was still a young boy, the major part of the food-getting tasks fell on my shoulders. My father stayed back in the 'house' to guard it against anyone coming and taking over our place, do the basic house chores and talk to people to get information on what was happening in town.

So, we had lived like this—existed like this, would be a more appropriate way to describe it—already for a couple of months and because it was now July, that is, the mid-summer in Europe, it was much easier than if it had been winter.

Several weeks after we first occupied 'our house' we were joined by a family of four, namely husband, wife and two young boys, about 4 and 5 years old. He was a White Russian and she was a Serbian woman who in her childhood lived in USA, and could still speak 'American' quite well. She did the laundry for the soldiers and he looked after the children and did the housework.

Some inhabitants in Asten, 1947

My father and he got on well together, as seen in the group photo taken about two years later in a camp. My father is in the back row flanked by two women. The father of the family is the third on the left, while his wife is in the centre first row, with their two little sons and a young friend in the front. Interestingly, I have always called the two kids Micha and Kicha and still remember that well. Actually, Micha and Kicha were the names of two boys in a comic series, so no wonder I remember it!

One hot day in Salzburg after 'lunch', my father and I went to Salzach for a swim and to do the laundry. Salzach is the river that runs through Salzburg and divides the old town from the new town. After the laundry-swim, which really consisted of getting into the water and splashing the clothing to be washed around, rather than actually swimming, we started walking back.

It must have been around mid-afternoon, because the streets were pretty much empty of people. As we walked, I saw, some distance away, on the other side of the street, a person in the same Luftwaffe uniform as I was still wearing. He had a rucksack on his back, and walked, or rather semi-marched, in a determined way in our direction. I said to my father, 'Look, there is a person walking there and he is wearing the same uniform as I am.' As he approached nearer, I could see him a bit clearer and I said to my father, 'He looks like he is wearing glasses. I think it is Serge.' And so it was! Unbelievable. Absolutely and impossibly unbelievable!

If you think about us meeting my brother the way we did, it was nothing short of a miracle. Consider this: I saw my brother last about five months earlier in another country in an end-of-war environment when everything is confused and order is breaking down. Both my father and I did not expect to see him for a long time yet, if ever … and then right at that minute to see him in Salzburg, walking on the same street at the same time, must surely be a miracle. Like the chance in a billion of my meeting my father—so meeting my brother was a chance in ten billions. Just imagine, if I had gone to another cafe, or had the money to pay the waiter so he did not make a scene … and that's it. My father and I would not have met. And now, a matter of maybe 1–2 minutes difference, or us taking another route, and my father and I would not have met my brother. However, it did happen and so, again, the family was together!

As my brother tells it, the cadets were wearily marching to München, when the war ended for them, also in the American zone. They were put in a POW camp and not treated particularly well. The food was scarce, the camp was overflowing with people and the guards were tough. Somehow my brother escaped from the camp some days later and got to a farm where he holed up for couple of months, before continuing his march to München via Salzburg, which was the accepted route.

So, here we were all together in our 'house'. It was nice, but it also meant an extra mouth to feed. Sorry if I always seem to be preoccupied with food, but I was only a thirteen year old boy and still growing fast. If you've had experience with growing boys, you would know how ravenous they always are.

A few weeks after my brother came, my father heard that there was something being established for the refugees by the authorities. So we went to register and were put in a huge dormitory that had previously been a gymnastics hall and now held something like 600 beds.

We were in there for perhaps a month before we decided to move to another refugee place, namely, 'Lehner Kaserne' or 'Lehner Barracks', just on the other side of the Lehner Bridge across the Salzach river. The reason we moved was that it was supposed to be a better place for regular food. Unfortunately, many other people must have thought the same, because when we got to it there was no more room left for anybody new. But, not to fear, we spied an empty old ambulance van in the yard and we commandeered it as our new home. And that it was for about 2–3 months.

Lehner Kaserne ca 1946.

Recently, I came across a photo of the place on the Internet, as it looked at that time. The photo must have been taken from about where our ambulance lodging had been. As we discovered soon after moving to Lehner Kaserne, the place did not quite live up to its reputation as regards the regularity of food. However, although the living quarters—namely, the old ambulance van—was not quite the same as a brick building, we were on our own in it.

As the colder months approached, living in the van was getting questionable. However, before we could make a decision about what to do next, the refugees in the Lehner Kaserne camp were transferred to a camp in Saalfelden. I suppose they needed the barracks for something else.

ᛍ

Ahh … Saalfelden! Many images are conjured up in one's mind at the name of Saalfelden—a town in the Austrian Alps famous throughout the world for its superb skiing fields and breathtaking scenery. In ordinary times, this would have been a fantastic place to be; a famous resort, five star hotels, superior restaurants, superb cuisine, Wiener schnitzel with braised new potatoes, or pick your own menu, and so on. But this was just a few months after the end of the war, with shortages in just about everything useful, let alone desired, you can think of.

And getting there from Salzburg … well, it was Bela Crkva to Eger all over again, except the wagons were cattle wagons and not coal wagons as before. Nevertheless, it was still primitive travelling. There were families—men, women and children—all together; maybe not as packed as during the war, but the toilet facilities were still the night cans, as then. Sure, the journey was a bit shorter—two days, or so—but there still should have been some comfort stops at proper railway stations.

When we arrived in Saalfelden, we were trucked to the camp and installed in the huts there. I should point out that the American authorities decided to segregate the refugees of different nationalities into different camps. I don't know the real reason, but an advantage of this, that I discovered later on, was that you knew exactly which soccer team was yours and the one you should barrack for in inter-camp competitions.

Imagine if each camp was of mixed nationalities and you were, say, a Yugoslav and there were Yugoslavs in both teams. Which team would you barrack for? It just wouldn't work, and that's that! If, on the other hand, the Yugoslav camp's team was playing the Polish camp's team, there is no confusion as to which team is your team. However, I don't think that's quite what the American authorities had in mind when they did it initially. So, we were sent to Saalfelden because we were formally Yugoslavs and Saalfelden was a nominated Yugoslav refugee camp.

We were there not more than a couple of weeks when the snow started falling and the winter set in a bit earlier than was expected, so we were told. And it was one of the harshest on record. Just our luck! The American soldiers got the local workshops to build plywood structures with windows and doors for their open army jeeps so they would be kept warm. Of course, there was neither room, nor then the need any more, for the machine gun that was the standard part of a combat jeep.

With all that snow, Saalfelden and its surrounds looked absolutely magnificent—a picture card resort. Shame we were too busy surviving the cold to pay much attention to the picturesque beauty all around us. The snow was exceptionally heavy. In some streets that were cleared of snow, you were driving in a canyon with snow walls on either side intermingled with houses.

One thing that stands in my mind, and this was repeated in subsequent camps, is the life of families intermingled with single people—all in one long hut of some 60–70 bodies. The beds were never less than two tiers, so one would think there could be no privacy. However, it was amazing to see how people's ingenuity could ensure the propagation of species as dictated by Darwin's theory. People used blankets as curtains to achieve privacy and for this purpose bunks were just ideal!

ℊ

I could half-start this section as I started the previous one, because that would describe our next destination, Markt Pongau, well ... but I won't. Incidentally, at that time the place was always referred to as Pongau and not Markt Pongau. I would just say that for some reason, as we were just getting used to Saalfelden, we got moved to another Yugoslav camp in Pongau—a town half way between Saalfelden and Salzburg, but just as freezing. In fact, in the night time the timber supporting the roof of the huts often made very loud noise as the water trapped in it began to freeze and the resultant ice expanded and cracked the timber. In Pongau we went skiing in the nearby hills for recreation. It was a pretty boring life for young boys in these camps in winter, so any diversion was welcome.

Yes, about the food in Pongau: although regular, it was still insufficient. My father did the cooking in our part of the room which had a curtain separating it from the other parts. Thinking back, it was a dangerous activity. Because so much current was drawn by the spiral wire hotplate, called 'resho', the fuses used to blow all the time. To prevent that, people used nails instead of the fuse wire causing the fuse box and wires to glow bright red, especially in the dark of the evenings!

I must mention one cooking episode of my father's that stands out in my mind. My father had procured a kilo of potatoes somewhere and he was going to cook us fried potatoes to go with a bit of sliced silverside that he had also obtained. For this he took out a frying pan that had seen better days and had been used quite extensively for frying this and that, so its inside was not shiny anymore, but was quite dark and kind of oily looking. As my father had already used up all our oil quota he did not have any oil to fry the potatoes. Never mind, he thought, the frying pan looked oily enough and he proceeded to fry the potatoes by putting some water in the pan to 'extract' the oil from it, which would then 'fry' the potatoes. He never lived that one down! I must add in passing that in my lifetime I have seen many people who were not scientifically nor technically literate, but my father had absolutely no nouse for anything scientific or technical, whatsoever. I guess that's why he picked law—and I believe he was good at that.

We saw the freezing winter end in Pongau and soon after, we were again transferred to another camp in Puch—a town near Salzburg and very near the river Salzach. In fact, our camp backed onto some woods we could walk through and reach the river. As in previous camps, we lived in a hut with other families or people, so it was male and female together and, of course, the children of various ages.

As before, the families put up curtains of one sort or another around their part, so they could call that a 'home'. But, of course, you could hear everything that went on behind the curtain even if you couldn't see anything. However, by now I was well and truly used to communal living and considered it normal—what, starting in the Cadet School in 1942 and doing it non-stop since. In fact, I had difficulty adjusting to normal living when it eventually came in 1952. So, that's ten years of community living, and the ten years of my formative life at that!

One unusual 'medical' activity that I saw a number of times 'next door', meaning the family enclosure next to us, was the man of the 'house', who came from a mountain village in western Yugoslavia, 'letting blood' from his leg to cleanse the body of everyday poison and make himself healthy. I can still see his wife, a skinny woman, scurrying around to his orders: 'Now do this!', 'Take this away and bring that thing here!', 'No, not that, you silly woman, this!' ... and so on. Generally, their children were somewhere else playing. I guess they had seen this activity many times and it was no longer anything strange to them. In fact, after watching this activity a couple of times I soon decided it was much more entertaining to join their kids to play.

In Puch my brother and I continued our idle life and spent much of the time playing with other kids and generally making a nuisance of ourselves for everyone else. I learned table tennis in Puch and, of course, continued to play soccer which was the principal recreation in camps for both young and old.

One event I remember very well was when I decided to build a boat to row in the river at the other side of the woods I mentioned above. It was a big project. I searched for suitable wooden planks, nails, saw and hammer, and when I assembled them all I started putting the planks together in a form of a boat. As I was building it and it started taking shape, many people thought I was building a coffin and made jokes about it. Still, I persevered; a flat bottomed boat is, by design, very nearly the shape of a coffin and I was building a flat bottomed boat.

When I finished building the boat, my brother and some other boys helped me take it to the river for a test run. I must hang my head in shame because the jolly thing filled with water very fast and would have sunk had the test not have been done in the shallows. OK, back to the drawing board, as they say.

Some men who saw the whole sorry episode suggested coating

the outside of the boat with tar. No sooner said than done. I got some tar from the camp workshop and coated the boat—and myself! Then we again took the boat to the river for a new test run and 'Eureka' it worked. The boat floated well; just a small leak, but nothing that could not be readily fixed.

But, as I said, I got myself covered with tar and it had to be washed off before I could go back to the hut. I went to the camp garage and got some petrol, but that didn't work. Then I tried scrubbing it off with sand—silly boy! That sort of worked but it also took my skin off. So, after many unsuccessful attempts somebody suggested I try butter. We did not actually have butter, but had margarine and that did work. Of course, now that I know basic organic chemistry I understand why petrol would not work and why margarine was successful. In fact, if I got some mineral turps, it would have worked as well and been much more useful—in the sense that I could spread margarine on my bread, but not mineral turps.

¶

Time marched on in these camps and in Puch my father was beginning to be concerned that my brother and I hadn't contin-ued our schooling since leaving Bela Crkva. He found out that in Salzburg there was a Russian refugee camp called Parsch—actu-ally a suburb of Salzburg—in which the émigrés had started a school approved by the American and Austrian authorities as a Realgymnasium, or in other words a classical high school as opposed to, for example, a technical high school. So, my brother and I went there. There we lived in a hut that was very similar to the single storey house I and the other cadets lived in Bela Crkva, except that there was no need for the 'parashas' as there was a proper toilet and a bathroom in the hut. Thank goodness for that! I could not have enjoyed my stay there otherwise.

In this 'boarding hut', as I will call it, because it was essentially that, there were also some of our cadet friends from the Cadet School in Bela Crkva and it was something like a reunion for all of us. One of the cadets there was none other than Michael Gontcharow, one of my two accomplices in the sabotage of the 'Savoia Marchetti' planes in Eger. I am putting it in this sensational style to remind people that it actually happened and that sabotage was punishable by death, but we were still alive. I must note that I say 'we' which includes Michael Chernyi, the third accomplice, but his whereabouts at that time were unknown. Many years later I heard that he was in Venezuela, but I have never checked that.

While I am on this subject, let me give the last information about Michael Gontcharow. He did not stay very long in Parsch, but joined the French Foreign Legion, so he must have been older than I thought, or just falsified his birth certificate.

I received several letters from him from what was then the French Indo-China, now Vietnam and Laos, and from Algiers which along with Morocco, also used to be French. When he was promoted to sergeant, which must have been in record time(!), he sent me his photo which I include here. The inscription on the back reads: 'For a long, good and unforgettable memory to the cadet and a friend Nikolaj Stanishewski from the cadet in a far, quiet and deaf (sic) Africa. Sargent Gontcharov. 26-1-1948. Sidi-Bel-Abbes, Algiers, Africa.'

However, the latest letter from him that I received was not from him directly, but from his lawyer in late 1960, when I was already in Australia, saying that Michael was in jail in Marseilles and would I send his fees to him. He did not say why Michael was in jail, but it was serious. I cannot imagine that Michael liked the Eger jail so much that he wanted to go to another jail!

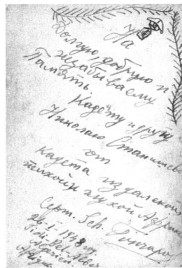

(Left) Michael Gontcharov in 1948, (Right) The back of the photo

In Parsch I also met Gabriel Sodbinow, who also miraculously met up with his older brother George. George was marching from Gmünd to München with my brother and the rest of the cadet unit. The two pairs of us, that is, George and Gabriel, and my brother and I, had a very long association extending, as will be seen later, to our early Australian years.

So, my brother and I went to the high school in Parsch, he in 4th year and I in 3rd year. These were the years we would have started in September 1944 in Bela Crkva had the world events not interrupted it.

While we were in Parsch our father was still in Puch. For some reason, he remained with the Yugoslav refugee camps and never lived in Russian refugee camps. This is strange, as he was Russian through and through. In fact, as I mentioned earlier in these memoirs, he spoke Serbo-Croatian language with a heavy accent. I don't remember that he ever explained, or talked at all about why he chose to be with Yugoslavs.

Our life in Parsch was a routine school children's one. Each day, including Saturdays, classes started at 8 o'clock in the morning and continued until 3 o'clock in the afternoon. There was a lot of homework and most of our out-of-school time was spent on it. On Sundays, there was soccer and/or going to the nearest picture show just over the hill, or to the 'Salzburg Altstadt', the old Salzburg across the river Salzach, to visit the museum, which I liked to do very much.

The food in the camp was passable and, since the camp—in fact all refugee camps—was taken over by UNRRA (United Nations Refugee Rehabilitation Agency) it was getting to be regular, too. There was a camp kitchen and a mess hall in Parsch, with tables and chairs where we ate in sittings because the hall was too small to accommodate the thousand-plus camp inhabitants all at once. For some reason, the camp was short of cutlery, and I remember the routine as the previous sitting was going out and our sitting was going in, the last remnants of food on the spoons would be licked off and the spoons passed over to us to be used. And, of course, the routine was repeated as our sitting came out. As this practice is a classic textbook way of spreading infectious diseases, I wonder why we never got seriously sick.

ʒ

After we were about six months in Parsch, my father was transferred from Puch to a Yugoslav camp in Asten near Linz—very much further from Salzburg—and then he asked us to join him because there was a school in the camp where my brother and I could continue our studies. We did that, but soon found that the school was nowhere near the standard of the one in Parsch. I remember the lady teacher of chemistry, who often used to remind the class, 'I am the daughter of a General of the Royal

Yugoslav Army,' which was OK, but her explanation of molecules was not. In fact, she used to pronounce it as 'male kule' which was the Serbo-Croatian for 'little towers'—and which was also her explanation of what molecules were! After that I don't think we were in Asten long before we returned to Parsch.

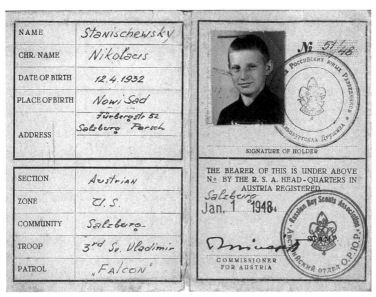

My railway concession pass.

Before I return to Parsch, let me say that both my brother and I, sometimes together and sometimes on our own, returned to Asten from time to time, especially during school holidays. So, one may say Asten was 'our home' and my brother and I were in boarding school in Parsch and this would be an accurate enough description of our life at that period. In connection with my travel to Asten—which was not on a railway line, but on a highway from Linz to Vienna—I had to walk some 5 km or so to the nearest railway station (Sankt Florian) to catch the train to Salzburg. Because I was a high school student I got a concession ticket, but had to produce my concession pass first.

One school holidays in Asten I got a job in the camp garage. In my six weeks there I learned quite a bit about car engines of the simple type; not your fuel injected 16 OHV type with EFI control, and so on, engine. They were the old side valve engines, no electronics and no gimmicks—just plain down to earth internal combustion engines.

One of my jobs was to do 'valve grinding', manually, of course! I certainly learned a lot about valve grinding, and also all about the muscles in one's arm and how tired they can get. In connection with my job in the garage, I started a two weeks automotive electrics course in Asten, but did not finish it as I had to go back to Parsch. Interestingly, I still have some of the notes I took then and all I can say is that my handwriting now is absolutely atrocious compared with what it was then.

At other shorter times when I came to Asten I went by bus to Enns. This is, a town about 20 km or so from Asten and on the river Danube which was the border separating the American and the Soviet Zones in Austria. It was only a few years later that Austria was unified, as per the Allied Armies Agreement in Potsdam. It took another thirty years or so for the East and West Germany to do the same.

At other times, I remember sitting on the side of the highway that ran near the camp, with my brother looking at the passing cars. At that time there were not too many cars on the highway compared with trucks and that was, of course, understandable because the country was in the process of being rebuilt and all the building material that was needed had to be trucked from here to there. We looked at the 'modern' cars and wished we had one. Interestingly, we were not impressed by the American cars, but were by what, I think, was the Austin A-40. Funny that?

While we were in Asten, and in refugee camps in general, starting with Lehner Kaserne in Salzburg, there were representatives from different countries coming to select appropriate refugees that could be accepted by their country as migrants. I remember in Lehner Kaserne we put our names down for USA and we heard from others that their requirement was for construction workers, so several of us spent hours walking up and down the stairs sliding our palms on the handrail to build calluses on them. Unfortunately, we did not even make the short list, so we had sore hands for days for nothing!

As a rule, people put their names down for every country that came along because the priority was to get out of Europe and start a new life. Everybody hoped they would be accepted by USA as migrants because we believed, and we could see by what their soldiers had in comparison with British, for example, that it was a rich country—and no doubt it was.

In Asten I remember the Canadian officials giving us a 'hammer test'. This involved asking you to make your biceps as hard as you could and then hitting them with a special hammer to see how high the hammer bounced. As they were after migrants to work as lumber jacks, I guess it was OK. I also remember that we missed out on Brazil, Argentina, Venezuela and New Zealand. It was also clear that these countries wanted able bodied men, or tradesmen of one sort or other. Hence, I started the auto electrician's course as I already mentioned, but did not complete it because I had to go to Parsch.

❡

As I already noted, during our stay in Austria my brother and I spent more of our time in Parsch than in any other camp, and that was understandable because we were going to school there. I worked hard at my school studies and tried to make up for lost time. My brother, on the other hand, coasted along. So the result was that at the start I was one year behind him, then later I was in the same year as him and eventually, in 1949, I was one year ahead of him and in the final year of high school. In the class photo my brother and I were in the same year. I am right in the front and my brother is standing right at the back. The photo also includes George Sodbinow. Gabriel was in the class below us.

Parsch class photo

We did not have school uniforms because it was not required, nor were they something that could be found in any clothing shop. After all, it was just after the war and shortages in most items were still hard felt. Of course, black market was still operating strongly in 1949, but the focus was now switched from the basic food items to the more up-market items, like nylon stockings, French perfume, Swiss watches, and so on.

Even with my accelerated school studies, I was still able to maintain very good results—in fact I made the marble plaque, or the honours board, as it is known in Australian schools, in the foyer of the school each year.

My Draughtsman's Certificate

I also did coaching of a few students in the year below to earn some money and on top of all this I did an evening course in Draughtsmanship to get a useful 'trade' for migration to another country. My Draughtsmanship certificate is in English and Spanish, and shows a photo of me at that time.

Looking at it now, I can see the strain of all that hard work and long hours on my face. The photo was taken in 1949 and if you compare it with the class photo, taken less than a couple of years earlier, the difference is really tremendous. I was certainly pushing myself then and, I guess, ever since. Or is it just me as me!

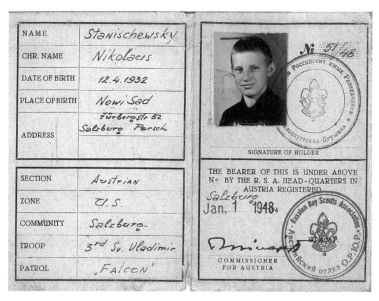

My Scout ID.

You wouldn't believe this, but as if all this was not enough to keep me occupied, I was also involved in other activities, namely:

1) <u>Scout Movement,</u> as per my ID Card where I reached the rank of 'Eagle Scout' which is, I think, something like a 'Queen's Scout',

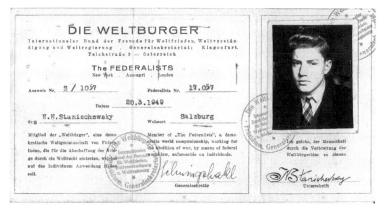

My World Citizen ID

2) <u>World Citizen Movement</u> using Esperanto which was then a very popular language, and I even learnt to speak it in a fashion. It was an international language developed by an American teacher, who must have been an expert in languages, in their origin and in their construction, because Esperanto is a very simple language, indeed. The grammar rules are almost non-existent and the words themselves are mainly those of Latin and Spanish—the two 'corner stone' languages. Unfortunately, parochial nationalisms prevailed, people were not far-sighted enough and it did not catch on. Just imagine, now with United Europe, multinationals, World Bank and the world shrinking fast, everybody could have been speaking Esperanto. It beats English for simplicity hands down! And no knowledge of spelling needed, because there is no spelling involved!

3) <u>Secret Society Movement</u> with its ultimate goal to liberate Russia from the Bolsheviks. Of course, we met secretly and I can't divulge much about it as, you would expect, I was sworn to secrecy. I assume the Society is no longer relevant as there are no more Bolsheviks in Russia which, anyway, is now a 'democracy'. I must say that I did learn a few useful debating tricks and mob control from the Society's training sessions.

4) <u>Nuclear Physics which</u> I seemed to have been fascinated by. I read everything about it I could lay my hands on. I still have some nuclear physics notes I copied from magazines. In fact, I had made up my mind that after I finish school I would study Nuclear Physics at the university. But, why I did not … that's later!

5) <u>Sport</u> also received some of my time. I played soccer and table tennis, and in winter time I skied just up the hill. The camp was at the foot of the hill.

So, I was a busy boy in Parsch. And when I went to Asten I took it easy, or rather a little easier. On our last trip to Asten around April 1949, my father had put in an application for Australia, and when my brother and I arrived in Asten, the three of us were interviewed, but this time my father had a trade certificate up his sleeve!

In our past applications and interviews, most countries would accept my brother and me, but not our father. He was a problem and, I guess, no country rightly wanted an older man—and a lawyer with political background at that! So, he did a two-day milkman course and received a certificate with an appropriate stamp and signature. I don't know what the contents of the course were, nor whether there was any practical component in it, like actually milking a cow, or what. The fact of the matter was that the Australian officials were apparently satisfied with my father's newly acquired skill and we were accepted to immigrate to Australia. I am sure we celebrated much that day, even if the only thing we knew about Australia was that it had boomerangs and kangaroos.

My HSC Certificate: front and overleaf

In the next few days we were advised that our departure would be on 25 May. My brother and I returned to Parsch to finalise our school activities and pack our belongings, which was not difficult as we didn't have much and it all again fitted into our rucksacks. We also found out that the Australian officials visited Parsch and several families and friends were selected, including George and Gabriel Sodbinow.

Because of the urgency of the case and my good record at school, I was given my final examinations—which in our case always were both written and oral—several weeks before the proclaimed date. My answers were quickly assessed and I was issued with my High School Certificate. Then, my brother and I went to Asten to join our father in our journey to Australia with embarkation in Naples, Italy.

¶

We left the camp in Asten in army trucks for the railway station in Linz where we were put on the train that would take us to Naples. The journey was long and tedious. Eventually, we arrived in Naples and were trucked to Campo Bagnolli, or the camp in the town of Bagnolli, essentially a distant suburb of Naples. Many years later, in 1987, I visited Bagnolli Steel Works and went by where I thought the camp was, but there was no longer any camp; instead the area was all units and more units.

Anyway, initially the timetable showed us embarking a few days after arrival in the camp, so we were full of expectations. However, we were informed that we may be there for a week or two longer due to a wharfies strike in Australia that was holding up shipping. Later we were to learn that all kinds of strikes were normal events in Australia in those days.

So, here we were, stuck in the camp in Bagnolli near

Naples—a famous city for tourists with attractions like opera, famous churches, the volcano Vesuvius and the buried town of Pompey being excavated. Incidentally, from our camp in Bagnolli we looked directly to the island of Capri, which was the hideaway at that time of Gladys Moncrief, the famous Australian opera singer—not that we knew anything about her or it at the time, or cared much, for that matter. We were too busy doing our own thing.

We were young and impatient. What did we know about Australia? Not much at all. As I noted earlier, boomerangs and kangaroos just about exhausted our knowledge of Australia. Oh … and that it was a hot, tropical country. So, here we were in Italy in summer time, warm and balmy weather, and a country with its famous wine and we had no money. But, not to worry, Australia is a hot country, is it not? So, why do we need long sleeve shirts long trousers and woollen vests. We'll never use them there! Sell them and buy wine. What a great idea! So, we had good time and with many sore heads to prove it!

Then, it was time. The ship had arrived and we were taken by army trucks again to the harbour in Naples for embarkation. Then … good-bye Europe. Hope never to see you again! We had too much suffering there and felt glad to see the last of it. That's how we really felt at that time.

The name of the ship was 'Skaugum'. It had been a German merchant ship, taken over by Britain as reparation and then sold to a Norwegian businessman who made it into a 'sardine' ship to be used to ferry migrants and had a Norwegian crew.

I said 'sardine' because at 24000 tonnes it was designed to carry 1700 people in large cabins with 3 tier bunks. The passenger list, part copied here, shows that there were 1672 of us and that the three of us were numbers 1368/70.

SS Skaugum
Departed Naples 4 July 1949
Arrived Melbourne, Australia 28 July 1949

0001 ABATNIEKS Anna
0002 ABATNIEKS Voldemars
0003 ABOLS Dzidra

....

1368 STANISEWSKY Nikola
1369 STANISEWSKY Nikola
1370 STANISEWSKY Sergej

....

1670 ZVIRDRINS-ZVIDRIUS Jadviga
1671 ZVIRGZDINS Aleksejs
1672 ZVIRGZDINS Vilhelmine

Soon after we left Naples—I cannot remember how it happened exactly—I was put in charge of the Dining Room and spent a lot of my time below the deck on this chore.

I remember well the first sitting. Don't I ever!!!

As per the existing ship procedure, things like bread, butter, sugar, milk, jam, coffee, tea, and, of course, salt, pepper, serviettes and toothpicks, were placed on the tables. Well ... you would have to have seen what happened to believe it. People were grabbing bread, putting a two centimetre layer of butter on it and then as much jam on top of it as it could take. Then, half filling their cups with sugar and topping them up with coffee—the real McCoy, as they say, not your chicory kind! It was animal behaviour, but understandable. Everybody had been craving these things for years and here they were free for the taking. Of course, it was irresistible. I did it earlier myself!

I also remember stopping in Port Said and all the people in little boats hawking their wares and yelling a treat. The purchase of an item by somebody on the ship was amazing to watch. First there was a lot of haggling over the price. Then the item would be hurled up to the deck and the buyer would toss the money down, generally not very accurately, but the sellers were very agile and adept at catching it most of the time.

Next we went through the Suez Canal—and that was an experience, too, seeing nothing but sand on either side, most of the time, but sometimes also with camel trains.

Then, through the Red Sea to Aden where we loaded some provisions, including, as I later found out, oranges that had hardly any juice in them. Somebody sure made a boo-boo there (or money on the side!)

Then, of course, a long haul to Fremantle in Western Australia, which was pretty boring except for passing through the equator. This momentous occasion was accompanied by the traditional festivities and the dunking of selected people in the on-board swimming pool. The festivities ended with 'King Neptune' presenting every passenger with an appropriate certificate. It was fun. I still treasure my Neptune's certificate to this day.

We made just a short stop in Fremantle before continuing to Melbourne —our final destination.

At last we are in our new country and far from Europe. In fact, one really couldn't be much further.

We arrived in Melbourne early in the morning on July 28. Well, the boomerangs and kangaroos may have been true, but we were far off the mark about Australia being a tropical country! Remember what we did to get that Italian wine in Bagnolli?

My Neptune Certificate

Yes, we had sold all our winter clothing. And now here we are on July 28 in Melbourne in thin short sleeve shirts and shorts!

I didn't think I could ever be as cold as I was on that wintry and windy morning in Melbourne. The reason was that all that warmth for weeks beforehand had made my body more susceptible to cold than it would otherwise be. (I get the same experience now when I return home in winter from my two months stay in Indonesia. For a day, or two, I just can't stop shivering.)

So, in Melbourne that day I just had to endure it, until something would crop up to ease the cold. And it cropped up in two days' time in a small town about 300 km north-east of Melbourne: Bonegilla ... Home!

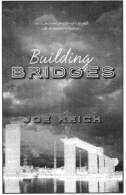

New Releases... also from Sid Harta Publishers

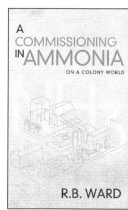

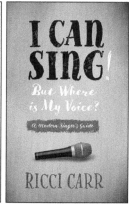

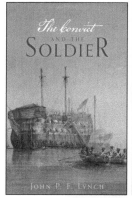

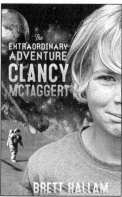

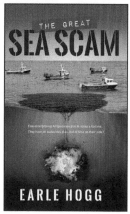

Best-selling titles by Kerry B. Collison

SID HARTA PUBLISHERS

Readers are invited to visit our publishing websites at:
http://sidharta.com.au
http://publisher-guidelines.com/
Kerry B. Collison's home pages:
http://www.authorsden.com/visit/author.
asp?AuthorID=2239
http://www.expat.or.id/sponsors/collison.html
email: author@sidharta.com.au

Purchase Sid Harta titles online at:
http://sidharta.com.au

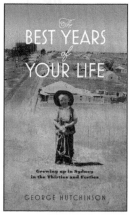

OTHER BEST SELLING SID HARTA TITLES CAN BE FOUND AT

http://sidharta.com.au   http://Anzac.sidharta.com

***

HAVE YOU WRITTEN A STORY?
http://publisher-guidelines.com